TWO SOULS
DESPERATE TO CONNECT
WITH HELP FROM A THIRD ONE

TWO SOULS

DESPERATE TO CONNECT
WITH HELP FROM A THIRD ONE

BY

LINDA J. ALBERTANO
ELIZABETH RAVER, PH.D.
AND
FRANK LUTZ

QUIET TIME PUBLISHING
Hollywood, California 90028

Two Souls Desperate to Connect with Help from a Third One
Copyright © 2024 by Linda J. Albertano, Frank Lutz, and Elizabeth Raver, Ph.D.

All Rights Reserved.
Thank you for buying an official edition of this book and for complying with copyright laws by not reproducing, scanning, or distributing any part of it in any form without permission from the publisher or the author.

LIBRARY OF CONGRESS Cataloging-in Publication Data:
Authors: Linda J. Albertano, Elizabeth Raver, Ph.D., and Frank Lutz
Title: Two Souls Desperate to Connect

Identifiers: LCCN

ISBN: 978-1-884743-14-6 (Paperback)
ISBN: 978-1-884743-15-3 (E-book)

Library of Congress Control Number: 2025900911

Book design by Kat Georges, KG Design International

Technical consultant: Alex Carmona

To learn more about The Linda J. Albertano Fellowship for Women Poets
go to **www.lindajalbertano.com**

Published by
QUIET TIME PUBLISHING
Visit us online at **www.quiettimepublishing.com**

Linda and Frank

Dr. Liz

TABLE OF CONTENTS

Preface i
Reincarnation iii
Beloved vii
The Love Ache ix
Introduction xiii
Two Souls Desperate to Connect 3
Dr. Elizabeth Raver Introduction 25
Vocabulary 26
    Spirit or Spirit People 26
    Heaven or Afterlife 27
    Channeling 28
    Light Trance Writing 29
    Difference Between Psychics and Mediums 30
    The Non-Physical Senses — The "Claires" and Telepaths 30
Science 34
Method 37
Opening to Spirit 39
How Does This Work? 39
A Message from the Spirit World 41
Bibliography 44
Communication Sessions 45
    Introductory to Communication Sessions 46
    01/29/2023 47
    02/09/2023 48
    03/09/2023 49
    03/14/2023 51
    04/10/2023 52
    05/01/2023 53
    05/04/2023 55
    05/24/2023 57
    06/23/2023 60
    07/27/2023 65
    08/17/2023 69
    09/12/2023 72

10/25/2023	76
11/15/2023	80
12/13/2023	83
12/28/2023	86
01/24/2024	90
01/29/2024	94
02/05/2024	99
02/21/2024	105
03/08/2024	108
03/20/2024	115
04/02/2024	121
04/17/2024	128
05/01/2024	134
05/15/2024	141
05/29/2024	148
06/12/2024	155
06/26/2024	162
07/10/2024	169
07/24/2024	175
08/08/2024	181
08/22/2024	187
09/04/2024	193
Frank's Article on Grief	**198**
Addendum	**206**
About the Authors	**210**

PREFACE

Two Souls Desperate to Connect: With Help from a Third One is the third of a series of four books about the life and work of Linda J. Albertano, co-written by Linda and her husband of more than 50 years, Frank Lutz. Linda is a multi-discipline award-winning artist who won recognition and awards in poetry, performance art, film and music, and was one of only a very few women who were ever awarded the title of Poetry Diva by the City of Los Angeles. An extensive partial resumé of Linda's work can be found on her web page www.LindaJAlbertano.com.

The first two books, **On the Life of Linda J. Albertano** and **It All Began with Cherry Soup** are primarily about Linda's performance, poetry, and prose, and include beautiful photos and associated collateral, as well as some of Frank's poetry and prose. Each book also contains information about Linda the person: where she grew up, her terrible childhood in foster homes, her excellence as a student and as a beauty queen, her move to Los Angeles, her achievements in the movie and TV industries, and how she met Frank and their 55-year relationship of love and success in their respective endeavors.

In the third book, **Two Souls Desperate to Connect**, Linda communicates posthumously with Frank as detailed in an extensive series of conversations recorded during sessions with renowned medium Dr. Elizabeth Raver.

The fourth book, **Poetry Diva**, offers a collection of sixty-two previously unseen works by Linda, discovered in late 2024 by Frank and his associate Alex. The poems, stories and songs range from the late 1970's to the first decade of the twenty-first century. The book also contains a few of Frank's poems referencing his longing for Linda, as well as a true story of one of Frank's international adventures.

We certainly hope that you, Dear Reader, enjoy these literary items, and feel free to respond at Linda's web page: www.LindaJAlbertano.com. To contact Frank directly, please email him at frankalutz@gmail.com.

REINCARNATION

Kora, didn't I meet you in
a previous lifetime? And
aren't you more than a musical
creature dressed in
skin and cowrie shells? I've seen
your supernatural harp strings
aim missiles of crisp sound
at our feet
forcing us to dance! (willing
or not.)

You play
with matches near our frail and
fatal happiness, singeing
us from root-of-hair to
tap-of-toe. One
day you'll burn us down to
red-eyed cinders.

Kora, are you the great-ancestor of
all music? Because I hear tones Celtic,
Gregorian, Bach, and Beethoven-like
roll from your stately
strings. In a previous life, you've sent
syncopated glory and Dixieland marching
down the ragtime streets in
our veins.
And in your wild
waveforms dwells a velvet-voiced
legend from Memphis, Tennessee.

Kora, the first time I heard
you, you bit
me with the bad juju. You grabbed
me by the hair and dragged
me into the deep
end. You flattened
me with cascade after crescendo of
celestial sound.
I learned to worship in the opulent
church of your holy
exuberance. Your sacred
music lines the ears of
God with extravagant
notes of grace.
You've caused hosts of
angels to weep. Their
fragile tears
burst into fireworks of sound
like a thousand tiny
goblets dashed against a
fireplace of jubilation!

Kora, I'm sure we've met before. I
recognize you in the whoop and
holler of banjos going. I've seen you
explode in the shake and
shimmy of every soulful, celebratory
stomp there is. I've met you in
the pop and snap of
rock and roll, in the flash
of midnight jazz. I hear
your Hallelujah Chorus in
the songs of the Georgia Sea
Islands and in every gospel choir
known to exist. They

daily sing your praises to
deities public and
powerful. And you
sass us back in
your native tongue!

By the way, didn't you and
your fingerpicking, backbeat rhythms
buddy up to
Robert Johnson and
Skip James?
Weren't you high-steppin' it
with Bessie Smith
and Billie Holiday?
Haven't you been found
in the DNA
of Ray Charles? Mingus? Coltrane?
and Miles Davis?
I even heard
you once
had an address in the
funky part of
Motown, as well!

Kora. We've met before. I'm sure
we have. We've
known you
in lustrous lifetimes
past. I've
witnessed the very
gods bend to the snap
and ring of your
irresistible strings.

Kora,
We've known you. In all
your famous forms. You're
disguised as calabash and
simple fishing line in
<u>this</u> incarnation. But you're
far more than a thing of skin
and shell could ever be.

Kora.

I know we've met. Yes!
Yes. Yes.

I remember now . . .

In lustrous lifetimes past.

Kora.

I <u>know</u> we've met before.

I never forget a face.

Kora.

by Linda J. Albertano

BELOVED

Thou art incendiary.
Thou sendest me up in sparks
100 times a day.
Thou makest me hum like 1000
buzzing phone lines yammering through
dizzy night.

When thou smilest upon me, I'm
money in the bank.
When thou snarlest, I am as a bad
check, bounced, and cowering
in thy heart's darkest dumpster.

Thou art the Lion of La Cienega,
the Rose of Sherman Way.
I love to lay eyes on thee.

Thou ringest through me sudden
and bright as fresh champagne.
My switchboard overloadeth.

Thy breath is as clean laundry
folded behind thy lips.
Thy teeth art as white Cadillacs
parked in neat rows.

I love to taste the texture
of thy skin.
Thine eyes art interstellar.

Beloved,
thou art incendiary.

Thou sendest me up in sparks!

by Linda J. Albertano

THE LOVE ACHE

I can't take her anywhere
anymore.
Not out to eat
at her favorite places,
nor to the movies,
nor to the opera,
nor on short trips
like to Santa Barbara,
nor to New York City,
nor to Europe,
nor to Africa,
nor back to Rome
so I can finish
my Vatican project.
I can't even hold her hand anymore.
Before COVID hit
three years ago,
we were planning Rome.
Then that plague
infected the world.
But as the worldwide infection
was subsiding,
in April of this year 2022,
Linda discovered a lump
in her tummy.
Off to the doctors
and the limits they gave her,
no surgery, no radiation,
only chemotherapy.
And so—she elected not
to suffer incapacitated
if these were to be her
last months with us:

who she loved and who loved her.
There, then started our
six-month journey
with the alternative care folks,
in Mexico and Canada and here.
But in August she was feeling uneasy,
to the extent that she told me
"Hankie, I might not make it,
I might die."
To which I cried out,
"No, Linda, you can't die!
I would rather die,
than to see you die!"
To which she cried back,
with wide open eyes,
"No, Frank, no—
I could not survive without you.
I would not know what to do!"
I had no response to that,
and only comforted her.
Just before midnight,
on Friday evening, September 2nd,
she was having pains in her tummy,
more than usual.
I took her to UCLA Hospital,
where they admitted her
and made her comfortable,
and took her into a nice room.
This would be her last place to be alive.
We loved each other more than words can express,
so on Tuesday afternoon, September 6th,
we got married—for the second time!
But that's a story for another time.
During the week that followed,
she worked in the morning constantly

on her computer,
typing new poems and new ideas
for new shows, into September,
October, November—
She was not giving up!
Then on Saturday, Sunday, Monday,
I could tell something different
was happening.
She was getting weaker,
sleeping more,
not working so much
on her beloved computer.
I was exhausted Monday evening
from not eating, not sleeping.
I had tried to sleep
in a very uncomfortable chair
by her bed, the night before,
but to no avail.
So at about 8:30pm
I kissed her on her sleeping head
and went home,
fell asleep in my clothes.
At 4:45am I received a call:
"Mr. Lutz, this is UCLA Hospital
calling you.
I am very sorry to tell you
that your dear wife Linda
has passed away this morning,
at 4:40am . . ."
I had no idea
that her end was so near.
In a daze, I drove back to
her room.
She was at peace,
beautiful, always beautiful.

TWO SOULS DESPERATE TO CONNECT

I kissed her on her forehead
as she lay in her bed.
Then I sat in the chair by her bed,
and took her hand in mine,
and I spoke to her:

> "Linda, I will always love you, I will love you forever. And as Dante followed Virgil when Virgil beckoned him, when you see my time is near, beckon me like Virgil beckoned Dante, and I will follow you. And I will find you again, my Love."

That would be the last time I will see her,
the last time I will hold her hand, until . . .

by Frank Lutz

INTRODUCTION

Dear Readers,

This is an unusual book. It contains the real-life dated transactions among three people between February 2023 and September 2024, all recorded and transcribed: a lady Ph.D. psychic-medium; a renowned and much awarded lady artist (in four artistic media); and the artist's husband and loving companion since 1968. What is unusual is that the lady artist, Linda J. Albertano, "passed on" in September 2022. But you will find out that she is still viable, that instead of being dead, an archaic term, she has "transformed" or made a "transition" into what is now known by science, as well as metaphysics, as the Afterlife.

The purpose of the book is to help people understand that there is, indeed, an Afterlife, and that communication with your Departed Loved One(s) is often possible and can be very emotionally healing. As the author, Frank Lutz, has experienced for himself, there are at least two ways this communication can be facilitated.

One way is via the expertise and talent of a qualified Medium. The other way is, after some instructional training and study, via your own use of the skills you will have acquired. Mr. Lutz uses both methodologies.

It is the sincere hope of the long-term qualified medium Dr. Liz, Ms. Albertano (wife of Mr. Lutz), and Mr. Lutz, that our efforts will help to abate the suffering and sadness of those who read this book and will put its principles to good use.

TWO SOULS DESPERATE TO CONNECT WITH HELP FROM A THIRD ONE

The genesis of this book was on Tuesday, September 13th, 2022. That was the day, at 4:40am, that my dear wife died of pancreatic cancer at UCLA Hospital in Santa Monica, California. The sincere aim and goal of this book is to help other people who have lost a loved one, and who want somehow to contact their dear one. Oftentimes a person who is grieving and is in severe emotional pain, like I have been, knows or has heard that there is a way to contact their loved one, but the grieving one does not know how to do that. This book will show you the way and help you to get started. It is based on my own experience and education in the science of Afterlife communication. It is what I had to do, and you can do it, too. In here, you will be able to read from actual transcripts, both written and recorded, taken from the conversations between my dearly departed wife Linda J. Albertano, our wonderful medium, Elizabeth Raver, Ph.D., and me, Frank Lutz.

My wife and I met on a very rainy and cold night in early February 1968. In fact, she picked me up hitchhiking, which was something that young people did in those days to help each other. The details of our first meeting will be told later in this book, and you will find them funny and fascinating. But for now I will give you a brief overview of our relationship that lasted over the next 55 years (70% of our lives!) and was/still is one of love and long-lasting devotion to each other. The point of this book is to show you readers out there who may lose, or have lost already a dear loved one, that you can continue your devotion to each other even after the crisis is over, including direct communication with each other. Through study and work, Linda and I have been able to do that continuously over most of the time since she has passed.

Shortly after Linda expired, I stood by her bed and bent down over her body and kissed her on the forehead goodbye. Then I sat in a chair beside her bed and took her hand in mine and remembered a passage from Dante. I paraphrased the passage, saying to Linda, "My darling Linda, I will love you forever. And when you see my time is near, please beckon me like Virgil beckoned Dante, and Dante followed him. So, when you beckon me I will follow you my dear, like Dante followed Virgil, and I will find you again my love, and I will love you forever." Then I kissed her hand and stood up from Linda's bedside and walked over to the door and stopped and turned around for one last look at the love of my life. It was not easy, because then I would turn away and leave the room and close the door behind me. It broke my heart. I did not know when or if I would ever see her or speak with her again.

When I returned to our home I collapsed on my bed and slept for hours and hours. When I awoke early the next morning only two thoughts were in my head: first, that if Linda is as desperate to talk to me as I am desperate to talk to her, then I must investigate and find out about this phenomenon that I keep hearing about called Afterlife communication and learn how to use it. Second, that I must do whatever it takes to preserve her legacy in the four arts in which she excelled, as in each of them she had been recognized and awarded honors: film, music, performance art, and poetry. I have accomplished much of each of the two goals I set for myself in Linda's honor; I have also written two books about her, and her poetry, and about our lives together. I still have more to do.

In this book you will meet three key people: my wife, Linda J. Albertano the artist, who is also my wife who passed away; Elizabeth Raver, Ph.D. a long-term professional medium and retired college professor; and me, Frank Lutz, author of two other books on Linda, namely: *On the Life of Linda J. Albertano* and *It All Began with Cherry Soup*. You will notice in introducing my wife I use the verb form "is my wife" and not "was my wife". If you are familiar with Afterlife communications already, then my use of the verb form "is my wife" will not surprise you. If you are new to Afterlife communications, then you will come to see that the Afterlife is a real place where we will go and where our Departed Loved Ones (DLOs) and ancestors have gone. It is a viable place of consciousness where life goes on in a different form, and I find it fascinating.

Between the day after Linda passed away on September 13th to the end of October 2022, I spent those 6 weeks or so organizing and /or disposing of certain of her business affairs and artwork archives and her personal effects. Her archives I have arranged for possession by an art/poetry institution to preserve and use as display and pedagogical material for the public. On November 1st I started doing my research into Afterlife communications and by the end of December 2022 I had read 14 books, including works on quantum mechanics science, parapsychology, medical research, laboratory research, and books by mediums on how they proceed with clients or, as they say in that discipline, with "sitters" (i.e., people who want to communicate with their DLOs). Since January 2022 to May 2024, I have read another 45 books on Afterlife science. I have also attended online trainings and classwork on the various subjects of the Afterlife world, taught by American scientists, researchers, and mediums from other countries, as well. Among my favorite professionals with various academic credentials, beside the aforementioned Elizabeth Raver, Ph.D., are researchers and authors R. Craig Hogan, Ph.D., a Near-death Experience (NDE) and Afterlife researcher; and Gary E. Schwartz, professor at the University of Arizona and colleague of Hogan; Hillary Michaelson, a medium and Founder and Director of the Los Angeles School of the Spiritual Arts; and Sonia Rinaldi, the physical engineer, researcher, and technician who has developed photography that is capable of capturing images of DLOs in the Afterworld, an amazing accomplishment.

    The persons I have mentioned in the preceding paragraph are the very best in their fields with whom I have had contact. This includes the two mediums, Elizabeth and Hillary, after I had dealt with several others. The personal research, reading, and classwork I have done in the past one and one-half years is in line with my academic background. I have studied in six universities, including three in Europe (France, Italy, and Germany), and graduated at the top of my class at UCLA, earning *summa cum laude* honors, and induction into the academic society for top scholars, *Phi Beta Kappa*. I also received a graduate fellowship. I have also done research in the Secret Archives of the Vatican, in the area of Medieval History of the 13th Century; I have a Vatican passport for research. But needless to say, it is not necessary for the average person to put as much time, effort and research into this science as I have done. What drove me is my passion and love for my dear Linda.

    At the beginning of my venture into Afterlife investigation and understanding, I determined to start with the science, that is, the research done on the subject by scientists. So, between the beginning of November and the end of

December 2022, I read books and articles on the scientific investigation of the Afterlife, among the 14 books I read during that time. I started with the subject of quantum mechanics, as I am comfortable with physics; it is not necessary for most people to follow my lead in that direction, as there is plenty of other great scientific research into the subject of the Afterlife. One essential subject area for anybody to understand is that of the NDE.

The purpose and goal of this book, Dear Reader, is to help you or someone you know who has lost a DLO deal with the grief, sadness, depression and loneliness of being in that position. I can help you from my own perspective and experience, and from what the professionals who have helped me have imparted to me. So, let's start from the beginning.

SOME OF THE VOCABULARY OF THE AFTERLIFE:

Afterlife, Afterworld – Not a religious term. Most of the scientists, researchers, mediums, and others involved in working to understand where we go after we pass on to the next life do not use the term heaven. The Afterworld is a place that is described as being much like the Earth in its beauty. It is inhabited by our ancestors, our DLOs, and others who once inhabited our Earth, but who have "passed on", not died. These folks continue to look like us, but with some changes. They have been "transformed" (i.e., they remain as a form of viable consciousness, that exists in a human like form) and the photos taken by the aforementioned Sonia Rinaldi look like their human forms. They talk and think and look like their forms. Scientists from all over our globe are embracing and studying these DLOs of ours.

Transition(ed) – The language of the Afterlife does not say that at the end of our life here on Earth we have "died" or are "dead". The language of the Afterlife describes that change as a "transition", or that we have "transitioned" or "transformed", because our consciousness has not changed. We can still communicate in our language, still function as though we are on Earth, and still look like ourselves! This has been demonstrated by some brilliant long-term researchers who have actually been able to get photographs of people in the Afterlife, researchers such as Sonia Rinaldi of Brazil, et al. She can be researched on Google and other places on the Internet.

DLO – Departed Loved One with whom you might like to speak or get information about. Could be a parent, sibling, relative, friend, or whomever.

Medium – A trained professional person who has psychic and intuitive capabilities to put you in touch with, or get information from, a DLO or other disincarnate person in the Afterlife, or to contact a Spirit Guide. Elizabeth and Hillary, whom you will soon meet, are both trained mediums of several decades.

Sitter – Possibly you, or someone, who seeks out and agrees to do a mediumship session with a medium, having a desire to make contact with their DLO.

Spirit Guide – An entity or spirit in the Afterworld who is there and/or here to help both DLOs and incarnate humans (i.e., us) to communicate or do otherwise. A friendly spirit. You might see the word spelled with a capital "S" for a noun or person, on Earth or the Afterlife; or a small "s" otherwise.

Soul {or Spirit) – This word has pretty much the same use and meaning in many of the languages of the world and applies in the Afterworld as well. At passing the soul leaves the body; your soul is thought to be mainly your consciousness, which survives the passing of your body.

Reading – An encounter between a sitter, a medium, and a DLO via telephone, in person, or in a group.

NDE – Near-death experience. The experience of dying, visiting the Afterlife temporarily, and then returning to their corporeal body here on Earth. The NDE person has no control over this event. This experience is medically documented thousands of times each year, in the USA and other countries around the world.

OBE – Out of Body Experience. The experience of dying, having postmortem sensate experiences such as seeing one's own body and motility while out of one's own body, and finally returning to the body.

ALC (or ADC) – Afterlife Communication (or after death communication). Essentially the same thing, just called out by two different names. It is the actual firsthand experience of communicating with your DLO, who is in the Afterlife.

Signs – This is an esoteric use of the word "sign" or "signs", particular to the science and metaphysics of Afterlife studies. A sign is something, or some object, left by a DLO in the presence of, or near, a grieving loved one here on Earth to let them know that the DLO is or was near them. The sign might be three small coins, or a white feather, or a certain bird—like a hummingbird or redbird—or a certain jeweled pin that was lost and now found—or other items. There is a short list of "signs" that can be found in some Afterlife literature.

Abbreviations in the Dialogues:
E = Elizabeth; E to L = E to Linda; E to F = E to Frank
L= Linda; L to E = L to Elizabeth; L to F = L to Frank
F = Frank; F to E = F to Elizabeth; F to L = F to Linda

There will be other definitions and sets of initials as we go along in the book. The above sets are the most prevalent and useful.

In most of my experience studying the Afterlife ethics and protocols, the language is pretty much kept neutral, or nonsectarian, which I believe is a good thing. Communication with the Afterlife has gone on among many civilizations and cultures and religions around our world for tens of centuries. Conversations with and instructions from the spirit world to mankind have been recounted in holy books, as well as in verbal lore on all of the continents. Jungle cultures in Africa, plains and mountain cultures in native America, the Sea Peoples around the Mediterranean and South China seas have all corresponded with their own deities and spirits for eons. So, this all is nothing new, except in today's world with our technology it is now more possible for all of us, not just holy men, to engage with the Afterworld and our DLOs in the Afterlife. It is all open to everybody, which is all the more reason that it be free from domination by any one set of religious beliefs, language, or dogma. In recent years, even the Vatican has, in public written articles and statements, lifted its former prohibitions against investigation into and dialogue with the Afterlife.

During November and December of 2022, when I first started my research into the Afterlife communications by reading 14 books in that time, I read about the science of quantum mechanics (only a couple of books) and the study of atoms and subatomic particles as they affect the motility of consciousness and everything else in the world; plus research about the NDE experience, which affects so many people around the world; plus research by the medical and psychology professionals; and experiences reported by mediums about their encounters while servicing their sitters and their sitters' DLOs. It is useful, but not necessary, for the average person to read about the science of quantum mechanics, if one is not comfortable with science, in my opinion. It is very useful to read about the NDE experience; also, about the mediumship experience that many sitters have.

During the last two months of 2022, when I was starting to read about the Afterlife experience, I was also finding out about researchers with whom I would like to speak, either over the phone or on the Internet. I also started to research mediums, with an eye to having my first mediumship encounter early in 2023, which I ultimately did have. In addition, I started taking an online course about mediumship, not that I wanted to become a medium, but I wanted to understand how they proceed in their attempts to help the grieving sitters who are in search of their DLOs.

During the first three months of 2023, I had several experiences myself as a sitter with various mediums, including men and women. These experiences were all eye-opening and valuable to me in determining how I wanted to proceed as a sitter and with whom. During this time, I was lucky enough to encounter Elizabeth Raver via a referral made by another professional medium. After a couple of outstanding Readings with Elizabeth and her great personality, gentility, and tendency to enjoy a good laugh, plus her intelligence and commitment to helping me communicate with Linda, I decided to continue with her, and do so up to the present. In addition to Readings, via telephone or in person, Elizabeth does online tutorials via Zoom with groups, and with individuals, about subject matter related to the Afterlife. Elizabeth is also a professor of Psychology, which keeps her very busy.

In addition to encountering Elizabeth during this time, I was also doing a lot of research online to find more sources for in-person or online tutoring in how mediumship works. I wanted to know step by step the procedure that a person must go through before they become a certified medium. During that search, I came to understand that students of mediumship learn about the difference between a psychic reader and an intuitive reader, otherwise known as a medium. I took courses in Transcendental Meditation (TM) in order to understand how to quiet my mind and go into a light trance in order to try to communicate with the Afterlife. After that I had another bit of good luck by doing online research with my computer and discovering a school called the Los Angeles School for the Spiritual Arts (LASSA), headed up by its Founder and Director, Hillary Michaelson. I have been studying with the LASSA for well over a year with excellent results in understanding the practice of mediumship. Like Elizabeth, Hillary is very intelligent, and has a wonderful, supportive personality. Hillary has a stratified and progressive curriculum that starts at the beginning level of mediumship and works up to the intermediary level, and finally to the advanced level and a certificate for those who want to become a professional medium. The entire process normally takes a year of regular classes and tutoring by Hillary, and can last up to two years or so, depending on the student's commitment to the course work. And believe me, you will find out things about yourself that will surprise you! All good!

Parenthetically, I want to say about Elizabeth and Hillary, both of these ladies are, like Linda and me, what I call "laughers": they have great upbeat and positive personalities, and are always ready for a good laugh, no matter how busy they may be.

The thrust of this book will be about my own initiation into the actual process of contacting Linda during sessions with Elizabeth, as during her sessions she both records our voice transactions on the computer and she also transcribes into written form those same interactions among Linda, and herself, Elizabeth, and me during the Reading.

The way the Reading works with Elizabeth is that on a prearranged certain date and at a certain time, Elizabeth in Connecticut will contact me in California via telephone. But just prior to me she will have done two other actions. She will have made a plea to her own Spirit Guide(s) for help and guidance during the Reading, usually with a short prayer. Also, she will have made initial contact with Linda or have tried to discover if Linda, or another of my relatives, is available. After this beginning ritual, she will contact me, and we will begin.

A couple of days prior to our Reading date, I will have emailed to Elizabeth a written list of my questions and comments to convey to Linda for this Reading, on one page. Linda often knows these details in advance, as she has explained to me that she knows what I write and what I am thinking, i.e.: she can read my mind in advance so the data on the notes I have sent to Elizabeth are no surprise to Linda. This is fine with me, that Linda has this access to what I am thinking, as she explains that she is always with me in mind and spirit, which is indicative of our love for each other.

After greetings among the three of us, and verification that we are all in contact, Elizabeth will start with what is on my written and emailed page. The items on the page of my notes might be about any topic: how and what Linda is doing in her new environment; what she may be working on currently, which could include poetry, music, painting, a community event; travel; friends she has made there in the community; her own healing; and so on.

The subject of healing in the Afterlife is an interesting one. It has been explained to me by Linda, and in some of the 60 books I have now read on all aspects of the Afterlife, written by expert authors from all over the world, that when people/souls arrive in the Afterlife, they begin to go through a process of both physical and mental healing, like what we would call therapy. Let's face it: when we pass on to the next life, it is usually due to the effects of a disease or accident, or the breaking down from old age, all of which can cause us to go through both physical and mental trauma. In the Afterlife, apparently provisions are made in the communities there for all new arrivals to be able to get over the effects of the trauma that led to their end of life on Earth. The healing process can last for an indefinite period of time, will differ from person to person, and can recur at various times of one's life in the Afterlife, as needed. The healing process is administered and monitored by professionals who themselves have passed over from their time on Earth. My Linda has gone through several periods of healing there, both for the trauma she suffered from the disease that ended her life here, and for the suffering she endured as a child growing up in unkind and uncaring foster homes.

In this book, we will begin our venture to the Afterlife with a brief description of the NDE. Many of you readers know about the NDE from family experiences, or friends who have been through it, or other stories. For those of you who don't know about NDEs, it can best be described as the temporary death of someone, and later, a complete revival into life again. There are many situations that can describe an NDE event: a surgical procedure gone wrong, and the patient dies on the operating table; an automobile accident, and the driver and/or passenger is killed; a fall down steps, the person hits the bottom hard, and dies; a sudden heart attack while the victim is sitting in his/her easy chair at home; and many other unfortunate circumstances. Medical staff is already present at the site of death, or emergency medical staff are called to the scene, the victim is examined and pronounced dead.

Says who? The car accident NDE victim describes his/her experience more or less as follows: "I knew I was in danger when I saw the speeding car coming from the opposite direction right toward me. Next, I heard and felt a loud crash and my body being mangled. Then everything went blank, I went out. After that, I was conscious again, but now I was in what looked to me like a hospital emergency room, but I was up near the ceiling, looking down at what I thought was my body, it looked like me! I could see medical people and equipment in the room, and people working on my bloody body. I could see all around, even into the adjacent rooms. I started yelling, 'Hey, I'm up here!' but nobody could hear me. So, I made my way down to the floor level and tried to talk to a nurse who was working on me, but she could not hear me. So, I tried to touch her shoulder to get her attention, but my hand went through her, and she didn't feel it. Very weird! Then suddenly, I started floating back up toward the ceiling. And then, things started to change. I seemed to be floating out of that room, and into a space that was both brightly lit and dark in areas. It was very comfortable, I did not feel afraid, I'm not sure why.

After a while, I don't know how long, I was carried into what seemed like a tunnel. It was dark, but not scary, and I was sort of floating through it. Again, after a while, I don't know for how long, I started to see a light further along at the end of the tunnel. A while later, the light got very bright, and I came to the end of the tunnel. I could see people standing there, people I knew, people who had passed away a long time ago, family. They were looking at me and smiling. Finally, I came out the end of the tunnel, and the people helped me out and onto my feet. They were all smiling and treated me very kindly, welcoming me. They made me feel comfortable. It was a beautiful place, peaceful.

After a while, I don't know how long, an elderly gentleman came over to me where I was sitting talking to some of my relatives, and the gentlemen very politely asked to speak to me. He explained to me that it was not my time yet to be there, and that he needed to send me back. I did not want to come back, but he said he had no choice but to help me on my way back. He then led me back to the tunnel opening, and I went into it, and fell asleep. The next thing I knew, I was back here in the emergency room, in pain, with you people working on me, saying you were happy that I was alive."

The above is a typical description of how a victim of an NDE might explain his/her experience.

This above is similar to the experiences described by a large percentage of the people who have had an NDE experience, in many parts of the world, according to researchers. In one of the books I read, it was stated that in the USA, with a current population of about 325,000,000 people, it is estimated that as many as about 70,000 people will have an NDE episode within a calendar year. That is an amazing number to me.

The salient point about the NDE, to me, is the encounter that the accident victim has with "people" in the Afterlife. Story after story is told by NDE victims about encounters with relatives and friends in the Afterworld. The question becomes, who or what is the victim at that point, and who or what is the familiar relative of the victim?

The victim is often described as the soul, or spirit, or a "discarnate" human being (i.e., having no physical body) of the former incarnate human being accident victim. That is, the soul has left the body. In the science, the terms "soul" and "spirit" are not used in any particular religious sense and apply to all of us. When the soul returns to the body he/she vacated earlier and comes back to life, he/she is a complete human being again.

The relative living in the Afterworld who is greeting the newly arrived accident victim is a soul who is devoid of a solid body, like all souls there, but who has a shape and face like he/she had when alive on the Earth. In descriptions I have read about in my research, and as told to me by my wife Linda, people there have human shapes and look very human, but have no "insides" like they did when they lived on the Earth, more like a holograph. So, what is the driving mechanism or force? The scientists say it is pure consciousness. The Gautama Buddha, 2,500 years ago, talked about the "all world consciousness" that inhabited each of us and surrounded us everywhere. When we are alive on the Earth we participate in, and are part of, the universal consciousness. When we pass on to the next life, our body stays here, but our consciousness continues eternally, to be used continuously. The Buddha did not have the technology to prove his theory, but science today can explain the soul as analogous to continuous consciousness, as with the discarnate humans who transition to the Afterworld, still mentally intact and functional. For the doubters, start by reading up on the works of researchers like Sonia Rinaldi, R. Craig Hogan, and Gary E. Schwartz, all long-term Ph.D.s and experts in their fields.

After I had started reading about all aspects of Afterlife communications, NDEs, Readings by mediums to help their sitters communicate with their DLOs, consciousness research, mental telepathy messaging, and so on, by early 2023 I decided to have mediumship events for my first attempts to contact Linda. I had already received some signs from her that seemed like her attempts to communicate with me. At one point, in the middle of a night, Linda actually contacted a dear lady friend of ours, who had been asleep at the time in her own home. Our lady friend was awakened by Linda's voice in her head, calling out my name and our lady friend's name. So, our friend was awakened, and recognized Linda's voice. Our friend is psychic, so she was not startled by Linda's voice, but instead grabbed a pencil and paper and started taking notes as to what Linda was saying! She took two pages of notes and called me the next day to read me the notes and email them to me.

Linda had explained that she had tried to talk to me in my head, a sort of mental telepathy, but my grief was so severe that she could not get through to me. This is a common problem with people like me who are in severe grief at the loss of a DLO: the extraterrestrial communication coming from the DLO is not able to get through to the grieving loved one on Earth. Also, signs in Afterlife communication are interesting to read about and understand, and I have received a few signs from Linda, which she acknowledged after I learned how to communicate with her. Most notable includes one time at 2:00am, when I was still awake reading a book on mediumship and Linda appeared in a low-lit adjacent room in a long grey coat and a grey hood, not unlike rain garments. She was only there for several seconds, and then disappeared. And no, I do not take drugs, medications or alcohol.

Later on, another sign came late one night was when I went into her empty room that had been cleaned and completely vacated and, to my surprise, right in the precise middle of the carpet were three American pennies, all with the date 2022 on them. Nope, no visitors nor cleaning personnel had been in the room, and I have the only key to it.

Another sign was at a Memorial for Linda on Saturday, December 10, 2022 in the back walled garden at Beyond Baroque, the famous venue for poets in Venice, California, in the afternoon. The master Kora player from Guinea, West Africa, Prince Diabate, was playing a solo tune when suddenly appeared a hummingbird flying around his head. Prince is a dear friend of ours and came from West Africa for Linda's Memorial. Birds were never seen before in the back walled garden of this venue. Hummingbirds are not common in that neighborhood. After Prince sat down, the hummingbird flew over by me where I was sitting alone and started hovering around a flower beside me. The visitation by Linda late at night, the three pennies, the hummingbird, these are all considered to be signs sent by a DLO to the incarnate loved one, in this case, me.

Moving on, my first few encounters with mediums, both men and women, were not very satisfactory for me. So, I decided to go on the Internet to research them, instead of relying on local referrals. I tried a couple of internet finds, still not happy. Then I saw an article by a man who had had a good experience with a lady who was a medium, and was affiliated with a university, and had a list of other mediums she worked with. I emailed and called the lady, who said she was very busy with a project, but she recommended that I call a lady professor in Connecticut, who was a longtime medium, named Elizabeth Raver, Ph.D. This was at the beginning of February 2023. We had our first session in March 2023. It has been a wonderful experience for Linda and me—but poor Liz has had to take calmatives ever since! (Just kidding.)

But I wanted to take a manifold approach to learning about Afterlife communications. I wanted to be able to communicate with Linda also on my own, on a daily basis, if possible. My reading told me that I would need to learn meditation in order to do that. Further investigation would lead me to TM, and a TM training center in the Santa Monica—West Los Angeles area of Los Angeles. I took a three-week course with that center, including online, in person, and on the phone, with a wonderful trainer named Denny Goodman. After that I took another online course, this time about learning how to seek out and contact your DLO, in my case, Linda. This course was with R. Craig Hogan, a longtime prominent name in Afterlife research, an all-around good guy who is devoted to helping his students go through his course with success. I learned how to recognize when I was on the verge of a communication via my TM approach, and how to "snag" it so that the other side, Linda, would know I was present, and that the communication was for real. Craig (as he likes to be called) helped me get rid of self-doubt, which he said is a common affliction among new communicators.

As 2023 headed toward the spring of the year, I took other online courses in communication with the Afterlife, but nothing seemed outstanding to me. Then, sometime before June, I saw online a web page that said "Los Angeles School for the Spiritual Arts" (LASSA). I read through the web page and noticed it was detailed and had a complete curriculum for training people to be mediums. I had no desire to be a medium, but I was/am very interested to understand the techniques of a medium in the hope that it would help me in my communication with Linda. So, I called the phone number and got the Director of the school, Ms.

Hillary Michaelson, who also happened to be the owner and head medium of the school. She was very accommodating, so I took a beginning online course, and another in-person seminar with her school. Since those first courses, I have also taken advanced courses in mediumship through LASSA, in a mix of online and in-person seminars, and personal tutoring. Hillary is an excellent teacher and has helped me progress to the extent that I have done Readings and some basic course teaching for new people from what I have learned in her school.

But my main focus is on communication with Linda, which leads to the main focus of this book: how Afterlife communication works, and its positive effects on people in distress who are seeking help. So, at this juncture I believe it would be a good idea to bring on Elizabeth, to get her perspective. Obviously, Elizabeth comes from a different perspective than my own. She is an educator, and in addition, she is a medium with several decades of experience studying and applying Afterlife communications, and helping many people who have lost a DLO or faced other crises. After Elizabeth, I will introduce you to Linda, my wife and best pal since 1968. After Linda, we will present to you real-life Afterlife communications taken from transcripts of the conversations between Linda, Elizabeth, and me.

One last sidenote: at the beginning of 2023, after I had already read 14 books on the Afterlife subject, I started looking for a way that I could learn how to contact Linda on my own, without a medium. I would continue to look for a good medium, who would facilitate the typical reading for Linda and me. This was before my good fortune to meet Elizabeth and Hillary. So, I took a couple of online courses via Zoom, but they were not very helpful. In my continued book reading I kept seeing the name of R. Craig Hogan, a researcher, scientist, teacher, and author of *Afterlife Communication* and *Eterrnal Life*. So, I contacted his web page, he responded, and wrote to me about his online course of several sections, plus some homework assignments, and his way to proceed. His course took me about three weeks to finish, and can take longer. Among the things I like about Craig's course are the fact that after each session he wants you to fill out an online summary section, in your own words, and that he gets back to you very quickly, to offer more help and tutelage for your continuing questions. Furthermore, and this is key, he sets you up with some exercises online with music and words, to learn to respond to audible signs or words you might hear when you are trying to connect with your DLO in the Afterlife. He counsels you against doubting yourself when you are learning how to communicate with your

DLO. Craig's course was the best I took and helped me a lot to communicate with Linda. Craig is an all-around good guy, and a pleasure to work with. With Craig's early help I have learned to communicate directly with Linda, without a medium, and have been doing so since early 2023.

Before we proceed to meet and hear about Linda, and from Elizabeth, Dear Reader, there is some information you need to know about the science we are discussing.

There is more and more physical scientific and empirical evidence coming forth each year, in many countries of the world, to support the information you will receive in this book. There are prominent, large, state-supported universities engaged in this research, in the USA and other countries, as well as in private institutions. Subjects such as NDEs, Afterlife communication, consciousness, and even extraterrestrial photography support the existence of a life after death. The research is not Bible or religiously influenced and promulgated. In fact, within the past two decades Papa in the Church of Rome (Vatican) has twice backed off the centuries-old prohibition by the Church against forbidding us from conversing with our loved ones who have passed and gone on to the Afterlife; articles published in *L'Osservatore Romano*, the Vatican newspaper.

Now, I will give you some factual information about Linda—where she is from and where she grew up, what she was doing in Los Angeles before and when we met, and a little more about how our relationship started. Linda is a very interesting person who accomplished a lot with her life in art and otherwise. After Linda we will begin our journey into the Afterlife communications, word for word as they have been recorded and transcribed, between Linda, Elizabeth, and me. I will describe our step-by-step process to show you how simple it can be with a medium to help you. The other way, that is, the direct communication between Linda and me without a medium, is a bit more complicated and requires study and work, as I described earlier.

Linda was born in the small town of Moab, Utah. Her father was a civil engineer and surveyor for the U.S. government. Her mother was an artist, doing sculpture, and landscape and portrait painting. At some point after Linda's brother James was born, the family moved to Denver, Colorado. When Linda was eight years old, and James was only four, the father abandoned the family. On his way out of Denver he did the dirty trick of going to the local "child welfare agency" ("welfare" is a misnomer!) and told untrue stories about the mother of his children.

The result of that malfeasance was that the children were taken away from their mother and put into foster homes—the worst part of that was the agency mercilessly separated the kids and put them in two separate foster homes! The two poor kids didn't see each other again for several years!

During her years in several supposedly "Christian" foster homes, she later explained to me that she was treated for the most part very poorly: no friends from school were allowed to visit her; she did not eat meals with the family, but was made to eat alone in her room; she received no birthday or Christmas presents; she was treated more like a household servant than like a child. Despite all of the abuse, Linda would graduate from Denver East High School as an Honors student. At the University of Colorado in Boulder, she would be an honors student and homecoming queen. She would be an honors student later at UCLA. At the same time, Linda was growing into a very tall (6'4"), brilliant, beautiful, gentle, and self-driven young lady who would later excel in, and be honored in, four arts: poetry, performance art, music, and film. But the result of all of this trauma during her youth was that after she came to Los Angeles, alone, at age nineteen, she would spend the next two decades and more in psychiatric counseling, due to the good grace and helpful financial aid of the various counseling agencies. One fine man, Dr. Tim Brown, helped Linda for over twenty years for little or no fee, because as he told me, he "believed in her." His faith in who Linda could become would lead to magnificent results!

In Los Angeles, starting at age nineteen, Linda worked odd jobs as a waitress and cleaning houses, and hanging out with the arts community in her spare time. She was "discovered" by several agencies for modelling and film, and continued to study music, making friends early on with such luminaries as the great American Blues musician, Taj Mahal, and others. She was hired to be the Space Girl at Disneyland, and for other promotional positions. She was hired on two occasions to be part of a USO entertainment troupe to go during the Viet Nam War to Viet Nam, Thailand, Japan and South Korea, to entertain our U.S. Military. As time went on, Linda would travel the North American continent, plus Europe and Africa, doing her poetry and music.

By the time I met Linda on a cold, rainy, dark, and windy Monday night at about 6:15pm, in February 1968, we were both just twenty-five years old. I had been seen by a Hollywood talent manager on the stage in repertory theatre at the Antioch College outdoor amphitheater at Yellow Springs, Ohio, in August

1967. That talent manager, Byron Griffiths, convinced me to come to Los Angeles, as he could get me work in TV and/or movies. I first came to L.A. in January 1968. By the time Linda and I met, we both had led spectacular lives. She was now enrolled at UCLA in the Film Department. I had been to five universities, including three in Europe (France, Italy, and Germany). I had started at age seventeen on a football scholarship to Ohio State University, got injured my second year, so I took a year off and worked in oceanography, and went to school in France. Between trips home to Ohio and abroad (Europe—more universities), I worked again in oceanography and sailed the seas of the world. In 1965, when I was at home in the springtime, by accident I got a job in a play as a stage actor with a local community theatre. That part led to an audition for the Antioch Summer Repertory Theatre, in Yellow Springs, Ohio, where I was hired, and worked during the summers of 1965, 1966, and 1967, again as a stage actor. In between plays in theatre in Ohio, I got a job on the stage in an Off-Broadway theatre in New York City. So, my theatre work led me to Los Angeles, where I met Linda—and my fortunes led to a wonderful life with her for the next almost fifty-five years—and thanks to the information that will soon be explained to you, Dear Reader, my life with Linda continues still.

I have written two books, recently published, about my Linda, her life in poetry and performance art. The first is entitled *On the Life Of Linda J. Albertano*. The second book is entitled *It All Began with Cherry Soup*. Both books are recently published. People ask me, "Where did you come up with the cherry soup title for the second book?" I will explain that now, before I introduce Elizabeth Raver, who will guide you into our discussion of the Afterlife science.

When I was ten years old and living with my family in Dayton, Ohio, my father started taking me to the opera house in Cincinnati, Ohio to see great opera works. Cincinnati had been settled by a lot of German immigrants, who established and supported the opera house. Dad loved great music and poetry, and when I was twelve years old, he and I were sitting in our living room discussing the arts. At one point he said to me, "Frankie, most people think that music is the highest form of art. But I don't. I think poetry is the highest form of art." I responded, "Why's that, Dad?" He said, "Because the point of poetry is to elevate the language, to make it more expressive, to help people express their emotions, and thoughts, and observations." Dad did his master's thesis on the poetry and writings of Carl Sandburg, the great American poet.

By the time I met Linda on that rainy February night, she had already been a published poet; but I had been writing poetry for all the years of my world travels after I first went to university in France. I never published any of it, as that was not my aim.

When I was standing on that corner of Doheny Drive at Sunset Boulevard in Beverly Hills, California, not far from West Hollywood, with thousands of cars travelling by me on Sunset, their horns aggressively honking at each other, I suddenly heard four loud honks behind me, and I just thought it was more loud traffic noise. So, I didn't even turn around to look, as the rain and wind were blowing from that direction, and I didn't want to get wetter. I thought her honking was just traffic noise in rush hour. Duh! But after several seconds went by, I heard the same horn sound, this time with four protracted, louder honks, so I turned around and looked. About fifty feet behind me I saw a late-fifties model Mercury coupe pulled over to the curb, body painted faded red, top painted white, and with a long arm sticking out the passenger window, beckoning me forward. So. I ran up to the car window and looked in—and saw a very tall and gorgeous gal my age sitting in the driver's seat with a smile on her face, saying, "C'mon, get in, it's raining!" The passenger seat was empty, so I got in the front seat.

At this time, in the late 1960s, it was not unusual at all for young people who are hitchhiking to be picked up by other young people who are driving, regardless of the hour of day or night, regardless of gender. At this time in history most of the young people were on the same brain wave in the USA: against the war in Viet Nam, and for human rights for all humans living in the USA, regardless of race. It was a youthful camaraderie all across the country. Linda and I were part of that.

I am just at 6'6" tall, and this young lady in the car seemed almost as tall as me, which turned out to be the case. I said, "Hi, my name's Frank. What's yours?" She said, "Linda," and continued to drive. By now I had forgotten all about my 7:00pm meeting with my manager Byron. Then I said, "Would you like to stop and have some coffee?" She said, "No," and kept on driving. No? No? Then I thought to myself, "Next. What do I say next?" Before I could say anything next, she said to me, "But I'll stop and have some tea and cherry soup with you." Bingo! Then I said to her, "Great! I love cherry soup!" She: "You know about cherry soup?" Me: "Yep. In between universities in Europe, I worked on Danish farms a couple of times. In Denmark, cherry soup is a national dessert dish. Cold cherry soup with cream." She: "That's amazing."

So, she drove us to a Greek restaurant on Cahuenga Boulevard in Hollywood, where the Greeks knew how to make cold cherry soup. They had owned a restaurant in Denmark, before coming to L.A. After about an hour and a half of talking with Linda, she dropped me off at my manager's house on Cahuenga Boulevard, in the Hills area. The next day, having no car yet, I hitchhiked through Beverly Hills and West Hollywood to the Franklin Avenue and Griffith Park area, to the house she shared with some other students, and took her to lunch. It all began with cherry soup and has lasted now for more than five and one-half decades, including getting married twice—with more togetherness to come.

Looking back at it all, it seems apparent to conclude that our relationship and love for each other over time was and still is, as Linda says, "preordained", meant to be, predestined. The fact that I was brought up by my dad and mom, who taught me the importance of poetry, such that I started to write poetry while in my teens, as did Linda. The fact that my dear parents taught me the virtues of a family, such as loyalty and helpfulness to each other, being fair to each other, protecting each other, being honest, doing your part for the good of the family. All of that helped me to help Linda. She published her first poem when she was nineteen. She wrote out of pain and a desire to escape it, to see a better world. I wrote out of adventure and a desire to show people what I had seen or dreamed. Then the way we met on that cold and rainy night: she could have kept on driving when I did not respond to her first honking, but she didn't. She waited for me and honked again a second time, louder and longer than the first time. We did not know each other at that time, had never met. I got in her car, saw a beautiful young gal my age, almost as tall as me, who turned out to be really intelligent and well educated. And of the thousands of cars going by that corner at rush hour, how many other cars, if any, could have had a poet in them? To top it all off, we both knew about cherry soup, and none of my American friends then or now have ever tasted it! Finally, here is the fact of our very long tenure together—seventy percent of each of our lives and growing. It was all meant to be.

In 2001, Linda was one of six poets inducted and inscribed into the famous Venice Beach Poet's Monument; her name and some of her poetry was put into the cement wall, reminiscent of Homer, and is there for all to see. She would also be named by the City of Los Angeles as a POETRY DIVA, an honor bestowed on very few women poets in Los Angeles.

More recently, Linda had been writing poetry and making occasional appearances before she died. Before COVID three years ago, I had planned to return to the Vatican to follow up on a long-term research project I had been doing and take Linda with me. (I have a Vatican passport.) We had been to Rome before, of course, and she loved Italy anyway. But alas, the dreaded COVID curtailed a lot of travel. Then, on April 7, 2022, early in the morning, Linda discovered a lump on her tummy. We went right into action, seeking both conventional and alternative therapy. We also went to Mexico, where we had sought medical treatment for a malignant breast tumor in 1987, which was successful.

That battle we won and Linda lived for thirty-five more years. She actually went on an Alice Cooper tour during that time, too. This time was different. We had been working hard, seven days per week with various therapies, to save her. Tests here and in Mexico showed that her cancer had already metastasized. Her last few months were full of desperation and hope, love and laughs, her always sweet and cheerful smile, great sense of humor, and poetry presentations in venues. She was very brave.

But at one point, less than two months before she died, we were sitting together talking when she said to me, "Hankie, I think I might not make it. I think I might die." I was shocked and jumped to my feet, exclaiming, "No, Linda, you can't die! I would rather die than you!" She looked back at me, with her eyes wide open big, almost fearful, and said, "No, Frank, you can't die before me! If you die, I wouldn't know how to take care of myself! I wouldn't be able to survive!" I was stunned, but silent. I could only kneel down by her chair and put my arm around her. Then she said, "When we are girls and young women, we are always taught to palpate our breasts, but they never mention our tummies. But we should palpate our tummies, too. Maybe we would have caught this sooner." Sometime later, in the hospital at UCLA Santa Monica, she told me she did not think she would make it beyond the next couple of weeks: "But I will be at peace, Frank. It's those who live on who suffer the most." And that is true, by my own account.

On the morning of Tuesday, September 6th, I was at home when I got a call from our dear friend and tax accountant for over forty-five years, Larry Johnson. Larry had called several times, always worried about Linda, who he loved. We were talking calmly, when suddenly he blurted out, "Frank, you guys gotta get married!" He was not usually so excitable and emphatic. I said, "But Larry! We did get married a couple of decades ago, don't you remember? We did that CDP thing, the California Domestic Partnership!" "No, no, Frank, I mean, really married, like a real wedding marriage!" Anyway, he calmed down, sent both Linda and me his love, and I headed for UCLA Hospital in Santa Monica.

I entered Linda's room at about 1:30pm. For some reason, the word "married" was in the air—one of us, either Linda or I, said the word "married"—like Linda, Larry and I were all on the same brain wave. I don't know what happened, but I said, "Linda, should we get married?" And she said, "Yes!"

The next thing I knew, I was on my cellphone, and I googled "justice of the peace who can perform a marriage". An 818 number came up, and I called it; a man answered it.

"Hi. Can you do marriages?"

"Yes, sure, I am certified. I have the license and notary stamp. Why?"

"I, we, want to get married."

"When?"

"This afternoon?"

"This afternoon? OK. Where are you?"

I gave him directions. I recognized his accent, as I grew up in a wonderful Jewish neighborhood, so I heard Russia and Israel in his voice. I am not Jewish, but I love them, and thought when I was younger, if I ever get married, I want to do that with a rabbi. I then called my French buddy, Jean Caby, who lives a few minutes from UCLA Hospital.

"Do you want to witness Linda and me getting married this afternoon for the second time?"

"Hell yes, absolutely!"

Jean showed up in one half-hour with a huge bouquet of flowers for Linda. At 4:15pm the rabbi showed up, a big guy named Josh, with a friendly face and demeanor. He spoke: "OK. So now we have to take 25 minutes to fill out this paperwork, after which I will give you the license."

After we filled out and signed the documents, Josh said, "OK. Now we are gonna have the marriage rites and ceremony. So Frank, you get over beside Linda's bed and kneel down beside her."

He then proceeded, "Frank, do you take Linda to be your lawful wedded wife . . . "

And then Linda, "Linda, do you . . . "

After the respective "I do" iterations from Linda and me, and a few "rules" of marriage from Josh, he finally said, "Frank, you may kiss the bride. Now you are officially married, congratulations!"

I kissed Linda, and we both cried like babies. Tears of joy. It was the happiest moment for both of our lives, truly. Jean Caby has it all in photos, thankfully.

On the evening of September 12th, I had been up for about forty-eight hours, running back and forth to the hospital, unable to sleep or eat, worried about the love of my life. I went home at 8:00pm, exhausted, and fell asleep in my clothes. At 4:45am on Tuesday, September 13th, my cellphone rang.

"Hello."

"Mr. Lutz, this is UCLA Hospital calling you. I am very sorry to tell you that your dear wife Linda has passed away this morning, at 4:40am."

In her room, I sat beside her bed and took her hand in mine. She was at peace, thin, but still beautiful. This would be the last time I would ever see her. Until . . .

Some days before she died, I told her something that I would now repeat to her, after she died. "Linda, I will always love you, I will love you forever. And as Dante followed Virgil when Virgil beckoned him, when you see my time is near, beckon me like Virgil beckoned Dante, and I will follow you. And I will find you again, my Love. And I will love you forever."

Finally, at the end of this book you will find a ten-page treatise I wrote recently about my sojourn into the world of Afterlife information. You will find it helpful from a different perspective, full of good information. It is entitled *An Idea for Those Who Grieve.*

And a final note about Linda: She was and still is a prominent poet, as I mentioned earlier. She spoke and performed her poetry over three continents. She was a wordsmith, and accomplished poets speak in very expressive and beautiful ways often; their language comes from their hearts. Romantic, passionate, effusive, declaratory, opinionated, and so on. So, be ready for a treat!

Frank A. Lutz, III
co-author, editor, husband.

Now, it is my great pleasure to introduce to you Ms. Elizabeth Raver, Ph.D. and medium *par excellence*. We will begin to show you how Afterlife communication works.

DR. ELIZABETH RAVER'S INTRODUCTORY REMARKS

When I first started working with Frank to help him commune with his beloved wife Linda, I never expected that we would be writing a book someday. Frank is very different from the usual sitter I work with. For example, by the time we had started working together, Frank had already read several dozen books on Afterlife communication. Previous to Linda's transition, he had never studied the subject; nor to my knowledge was he particularly inclined towards communication with the spirit world. Yet, within a few months of Linda's passing, he had managed to read several dozen books, had contacted several experts, and had worked with some mediums. I was a bit overwhelmed by his sincerity and grief. He came across as a man still deeply in love with his late wife. A man with enough courage and fortitude to continue his commitment even without her having a physical body. I felt I should do my part in helping him and Linda to connect with each other.

Unlike how I usually work with my sitters, a couple of days before each session, Frank would email me a very organized set of questions. I have to say that pre-prepared transcripts are not something that I normally provide sitters with as it is very time consuming. However, Frank does have, after all, a strong background in scholarship and I knew that he would appreciate my efforts. It seemed that the best way to address his questions would be to respond to each one in writing, several hours before our sessions. Then we could go over the responses later in the day during our telephone sessions. When I first started working with Frank, I had no idea that this method would evolve into something far beyond my original intent (i.e., simple question and answer sessions). For as our meetings increased in number, so also increased the transcripts' details and length to the point of becoming publishable. And so, that is how Frank and I eventually decided to co-author this book.

MY BACKGROUND

I have been sensitive since I was a child, but not until adulthood did I understand that I could communicate with the other worlds. During COVID, I retired from teaching higher education in order to focus solely on my mediumship. My formal training in mediumship includes various organizations in the United States and Britain.

I am not a certified therapist of any sort. My Ph.D. is in general psychology, which means research methods, not clinical practice. My dissertation was a phenomenological study of math anxiety. All that means is that I analyzed interviews of elementary school teachers regarding their experiences with math anxiety. My analysis did not require statistics. Instead, it required me to apply the ancient Greek practice of *epoche,* which basically means to be very open minded. In other words, through *epoche* I was required to set aside my own preunderstandings, preconceptions, biases, and prejudgments regarding math anxiety. In this way, I approached the phenomenon of math anxiety with fresh eyes and an open mind in order to capture its essence and meaning (Moustakas, 1994).

As it turns out, *epoche* was great preparation for my work as a professional medium. I gained invaluable experience that I now apply in delivering spirit messages as objectively as possible.

VOCABULARY

In this preamble to the transcript gallery, I would like to go over some terms for those readers unfamiliar with mediumship vocabulary. When it comes to mediumship, there are many different words and phrases that overlap in meaning. Needless to say, my perspective is not the only one on mediumship. Mediumship has been around for thousands of years, in cultures all over the ancient and modern world. There are countless numbers of words and phrases to reference it; this can become quite confusing. I can only provide and define terms within my own contextual experience. Please feel free to skip this section if you are already familiar with the following discussion.

Spirit or spirit people – For clarification, I will be using the word spirit or spirit people to refer to those have transitioned and no longer have a physical body. These spirit people now reside in a place known by many names including heaven, the other side, beyond the rainbow, etc. When I use the word spirit, I am not referring to the Holy Spirit, the Great Spirit, or even the soul (which is more closely related to consciousness). Instead, I am referring to the non-physical part of a human being (or animal). This includes their personality, their emotions, and thoughts, but does not include their Earth body. Hence, I will use the lower case "s" when using the word spirit to designate that I am referring to loved ones and guides in the spirit world.

In my own experience, I sometimes find myself struggling to find an appropriate phrase to describe those who have transitioned. This is not an easy task; in our culture, the English language offers many different phrases. In order to be as reasonably simple as possible in referring to the so-called deceased, I prefer the terms spirit or spirit people. These words do not have any negative connotations as do words like deceased, dead, expired, lifeless, departed, stiff, kicked the bucket, cadaver . . . well, you get the idea. To me, the term spirit people suggests that those without a physical Earth body are indeed still conscious. Usage of the term spirit when referring to those who have transitioned must always be contextual. Let's not confuse the word spirit with alcohol or some other unintended association!

Heaven or Afterlife – When I use the word heaven, I am simply referring to the place that people go to, after their physical body ceases to function. My concept of heaven is very different than that taught by orthodox faiths. For example, I do not believe that spirit people are floating around on white clouds playing harps. Nor do I believe that there is a judgement where newcomers who did not follow any specific religion will be punished. These concepts are outdated and do not serve well during modern times when we are seeking to better understand the nature of consciousness. Other words for heaven include the spirit world, the other side, over the rainbow, the non-physical world, the great beyond, the hereafter, world of spirit, Summerland, Florida, paradise, etc. If we tried to include names for heaven for different cultures throughout time periods, the list would quickly become infinite.

As science increases its understanding of consciousness, perhaps the word heaven will become obsolete. Until then I may occasionally use it because it is what I grew up with, it sounds more pleasant than many other references and it is simple. However, I will also use other references like the spirit world or the non-physical world.

Channeling – To me, channeling is simply the ability to sense and perceive things outside of everyday consciousness. Most people engage in channeling on a daily basis without even realizing it. Artists, actors, writers, scientists, inventors, and other creative endeavors often channel by tapping into their sense of inspiration. Engineers, law enforcement, doctors, and business professionals often rely on their intuition in problem solving. Even everyday activities can be considered a form of channeling. For example, gardening can be considered channeling as one connects with plants to sense what they need to thrive; gardening also channels nature's beauty thereby leading to a sense of wonder.

I do *light trance* channeling when communicating with Linda. I use the word channeling as an umbrella term referring to psychic information gathering about people, places, things, and events through the use of non-physical senses. This includes remote viewing, making predictions, psychometry (obtaining information about an object), locating lost persons/pets, obtaining information about crime, and aura reading. Mediumship occurs when channeling is extended to heaven to obtain information from spirit people. Stated another way, mediumship is the extension of psychic abilities to the other worlds. It is through channeling with Linda and other spirit people that I use mediumship to obtain responses to Frank's questions.

When I work with Frank, my sessions consist of light trance writing with his wife Linda, who is in spirit. As I will describe later, under the "Opening to Spirit" section, I channel Linda by relaxing my mind through prayer, a singing bowl, and meditation. This relaxes my mind from distractions so it can open up to the subtleties of spirit communion. This light trance is one of many forms of channeling.

To keep things in context, I feel a brief history of the word channeling is appropriate. The phrase "channeling" was first used by the famous American psychic-medium Edgar Cayce (1877-1945). Cayce is known as the Sleeping Prophet as he would seemingly go into a deep sleep during which spirit people would communicate. During his sessions, Cayce's Spirit Guides would speak directly through Cayce. This was not sleep talking (i.e., somniloquy). Cayce's dictations came directly from individual spirit people and not from Cayce. He was completely unaware of what he was saying while his body served as a kind of telephone connecting our two worlds. During such sessions, a secretary manually transcribed all channeled conversations. Cayce's work helped thousands of people in terms of healing, information about life after death, philosophy, past lives, etc.

Jane Roberts is considered by many to be the first well-known modern trance channel. Roberts published many different books based on her channeled communication with a spirit person (or a group of spirit people) called Seth. Judging by the millions that were sold, these books were very popular. Some may justifiably argue that Edgar Cayce was the first modern trance channel in America. However, Cayce's work did not really become popular until well after his passing in 1945 when, in the 1960s, books focusing on Cayce's mediumship began to surface. Robert's work in channeling began in the 1960s and continued until her passing in 1984 (Klimo, 1987). It is possible that because of Robert's success with her channeled work, people developed an interest in Edgar Cayce, thereby giving him long overdue recognition.

Light Trance Writing – When I channel responses to Frank's questions, I do this by simply opening my mind, heart, and body to whatever sensations, thoughts, and feelings I experience. The responses come from Linda or other spirit people. At this point, I am in a kind of light trance; one might say an altered state of consciousness. Words just seem to flow through my mind, into my fingers, and onto the document. It feels a bit like free association, daydreaming, or even the early stages of sleep when one is still partially aware of their surroundings. In America, many people call this automatic writing. However, some may simply call it channeling without necessarily discerning that writing is or is not involved.

In other places, Britain for example, automatic writing (channeled writing) is broken down into two categories. The first is called inspirational writing and the second is automatic writing. The British like to reserve the term automatic writing for when a medium goes into very a deep trance, as did Edgar Cayce, to the point where the medium is unaware of their surroundings. It is in this kind of very deep trance that a medium will write while completely unaware of what he/she is doing. This is the same kind of deep trance that Edgar Cayce went into except that he was speaking and not writing; someone else transcribed his words for him. The deeper the level of trance, the less there is of the medium's personality and the more there is of the spirit person's personality. From the British perspective, when I work with Frank I am doing inspirational writing. Americans of course, will likely say I am doing automatic, channeled, or trance writing. I usually prefer the term light trance writing or simply trance writing.

Difference Between Psychics and Mediums – Psychics intuitively obtain information about people, places, events, and things using their non-physical senses. Mediums do the same thing but are able to extend their information gathering to the spirit world. Hence, when referring to someone who can communicate with spirit people it is more accurate to call them a psychic-medium as opposed to a medium. However, because I like to keep things simple, I prefer to use the term medium. In any case, most people refer to psychic-mediums as mediums.

An example of a psychic ability is thinking of someone right before they call you on the phone. Another example is precognition, otherwise known as predicting the future. In another example, the police may consult a psychic for crime information using an object belonging to the victim. In contrast, an example of mediumship is when someone acts as an intermediary between the two worlds so a grieving mother can communicate with her late daughter. In this sense, my work with Frank is a form of mediumship.

The Non-Physical Senses – The "Clairs" and Telepathy – Non-physical senses can be broken down into seven types, often referred to as "the clairs". However, some sources may vary from less than or more than seven categories. The seven categories are: clairvoyance, clairaudience, clairsentience, clairambience, clairalience, claircognizance and clairempathy.

The clairs are not perceived by our physical bodies but rather are perceived internally, by our non-physical body. Some might call this our intuitive abilities. The ability to sense and perceive non-physically should not be casually dismissed. For example, a dream can be so intense that the dreamer feels as if they experienced it while fully awake. If dreams can be experienced so intensely, it becomes logical to accept the possibility that we can sense with something other than our physical senses. Most novice mediums that I know usually work with a few of the clairs. As they develop in their mediumship their experience can include all seven.

Clairvoyance (clear seeing) – Clairvoyance occurs when a medium experiences a thought picture of a discarnate person or object. In my experience, the seeing is not necessarily experienced by the physical eyes but within the mind's eye. At times, it is so well formed and detailed that specific clothing, hair style, settings, objects, etc. can be described. The spirit person can appear to be motionless and at other times moving. I have seen in my mind's eye a spirit person dancing, playing soccer, walking, playing cards, surfing, and a myriad of other activities. Each time it is different for me.

Some clairvoyant visions are clearer than others. This depends on the strength of the spirit connection and how the spirit person wishes to present themselves. By clearer, I mean to say how well-formed the vision is; sometimes clairvoyance can be very detailed, and other times not so detailed. The clearer the vision, the easier it is for a medium to describe what they are seeing. Usually, such visions appear as a brief flash seemingly out of nowhere. Through training it is possible to hold onto a vision for longer periods of time.

It is not unusual for a medium to close their eyes during a session, especially if the spirit's personality begins to emerge. Closed eyes can help keep the connection for a longer period of time. Novice mediums may feel as though it is their imagination at work. However, through patience and practice, they learn to discern between imagination and spirit messages. They also increasingly gain trust in the spirit messages they are perceiving.

Rarely, clairvoyance is experienced with the physical eyes, as if the spirit person were physically present. According to British mediums this is called objective clairvoyance. This is in contrast to intuitive clairvoyance which occurs in the mind's eye (Edwards, 2003). Although it is sometimes a good idea to distinguish between objective and intuitive clairvoyance, I tend to avoid making such distinctions; the distinction can lead to confusion especially when it comes to clairsentience which involves tactile sensation (see below) or for those not very familiar with mediumship. Besides, I rarely sense with objective clairvoyance especially when working with sitters. When writing descriptions about clairvoyance, I try to be as succinct and simple as possible.

Clairaudience (clear hearing) – Clairaudience is the non-physical hearing of sounds; they have a defining quality indicating their non-physicality. Similar to clairvoyance which occurs in the mind's eye, clairaudience is experienced in the mind's ear. From my own experience, psychic sounds are both subtle and clear. They are subtle because they require great focus and are fragile; distractions can easily break a connection. They are clear because I can perceive them with the same clarity as I hear physical voices, music and other sounds. They often have a pitch, cadence, volume, and intensity. Music is particularly clear, for some reason.

Depending on the quality of a connection, such voices can range in complexity from simple one-word utterances to complete sentences with a conversational flow. Sometimes during a conversational flow, I might fall into a pleasant light trance. When this happens, the spirit person can speak more directly through me.

Clairsentience (clear feeling) – Clairsentience is experienced through tactile sensations, both physically and non-physically. Physically, this includes the arms, legs, hands, fingers, back, knees, etc. For example, I might feel a pain in my knee, which passes very quickly, if a spirit person had knee problems while on Earth. Frequently, I physically sense a range of emotion in my heart and solar plexus. My skin may tingle, or hair stand up on the head, arms, or the entire body.

Non-physically, I may feel someone touching my hand or back. Medical issues can also be felt non-physically. I may non-physically sense my hands doing something delicate like crocheting, knitting, sewing, etc. At other times, I may feel my body moving, like dancing or running. I can also non-physically feel analytical activity in my prefrontal cortex such as math calculations, writing, problem solving, bookkeeping, etc.

Clairambience (clear scent) – Clairambience is the ability to non-physically sense an aroma or odor through the olfactory senses. In this way, I perceive scents associated with a particular spirit person. This includes flowers, cologne, smoke, water, etc. A scent can be so subtle that if I am not focused, it quickly fades before being noticed. In addition, a scent may be overwhelmingly strong or somewhere between these two extremes. When the scent is associated with a particular person who has passed it can serve as a form of validation from the spirit person.

Clairalience (clear taste) – Clairalience is the non-physical ability to taste food and liquids. This includes sweets, alcohol, soda, hamburgers, pizza, popcorn, etc. Psychic food sensations help keep sessions happy since food is often associated with pleasant memories. When thoughts and feelings are joyful it becomes that much easier for spirit people to communicate with us. For me, if I am hungry while experiencing psychic Italian pastry, it increases my hunger! Therefore, I probably should avoid mediumship when I am hungry.

Claircognizance (clear knowing) – Claircognizance is the ability to know something without evidence or logic. One just knows, without knowing how one knows. This is similar to gut feelings, as for example intuitive knowing. An example of claircognizance is when a young mother simply senses that her baby is hungry. Other examples include meeting someone for the first time and just knowing they are trustworthy (or not); finishing a friend's sentence; knowing who is calling you on the phone before seeing the caller id; and taking a different route to work one day, then later learning of a bad accident on the route you normally take.

Clairempathy (clear emotion) – People who are clairempathic can sense the emotions of others. Such people are sometimes called empaths. For example, have you ever walked into a full room of people that felt so full of tension that you could "cut it with a knife"? That is one example of clairempathy. Similarly, feeling another person's happiness or emotional pain are other examples. Researchers have found through surveys, that claircognizance and clairempathy are probably the most frequently experienced of the clairs (Wahbeh, McDermott, and Saghar, 2018).

Telepathy – I want to discuss the concept of telepathy because it is a common phrase. Some readers may be wondering how telepathy fits in with the clairs. The important point to remember about telepathy is that it involves psychic information gathering through mind-to-mind.

   A brief historical context may be helpful. The British Society for Psychical Research (SPR) was founded in London in 1882 with the intent of studying paranormal phenomena from a scientific perspective. It was the first organization of its kind offering the world a research-based view to explore a variety of paranormal phenomena including the clairs. Among its early presidents included founding father Frederic Myers (1843-1901) who is best known for his book *Human Personality and Its Survival of Bodily Death*. It is in his book that Myers is credited with defining the term telepathy as follows: "The communication of impressions of any kind from one mind to another, independently of the recognized channels of sense" (Myers, 1960, p. 11). Myers's carefully worded definition includes visions, sounds, bodily sensations, smells, and emotion. In addition, it allows for experiences during wakefulness and during dreams. In spite of telepathy being stereotypically thought of as only mind-to-mind communication, as per Myers's definition it also includes "emotions and impressions, rather than just visual apparitions or the transfer of thoughts" (Sheldrake, 2013, p. 191). In this way, telepathy may be viewed as an umbrella term for all seven clairs. However, as discussed in our next section, sometimes researchers make a distinction between telepathy and clairvoyance. Therefore, these words should always be viewed within their proper context.

SCIENCE

I would like to include a short discussion on some of the science regarding clairvoyance and related phenomena. I will not go into great detail as that would detract from the main purpose of this book (i.e., to share the mediumship transcripts regarding communications between Frank and Linda). Readers interested in science will probably like this section. On the other hand, I can easily imagine the eyes of other readers glossing over at the mere mention of science. If you fall into the latter group, please feel free to skip this section. I have done my best to make it as simple as possible. We will begin with Dr. Joseph Rhine and Zener Cards.

Joseph Rhine was an American research pioneer of psychic phenomenon like telepathy, clairvoyance, and precognition. In 1929, Dr. Rhine was hired as a psychology professor by Duke University. While at Duke he founded the Parapsychology Laboratory and the *Journal of Parapsychology*. Upon retiring in 1965, he created a private research organization called the Foundation for Research on the Nature of Man (FRNM). After his death in 1980, the foundation was renamed the Rhine Research Center in 1995 (McVaugh, 2006).

Dr. Rhine is well known for his research on telepathy using Zener cards. A Zener card deck consists of five groups of five symbols, for a total of 25 cards. The five symbols are: star, circle, square, plus sign, and three wavy lines.

To test for telepathy (i.e., mind-to-mind) the following steps are followed: The deck is shuffled, a sender chooses a card and then mentally sends the card's image to a receiver. The receiver then declares which of the five symbols the sender mentally sent. The results of such telepathy experiments are unaffected by the distance between the sender and receiver. Telepathy appears to operate outside the confines of distance.

To test for clairvoyance, the sender chooses a card and without looking at it, places the card face down on a table. A receiver then declares which of the five Zener symbols was chosen by the sender. This is a test of clairvoyance because it is object-to-mind, not mind-to-mind. In this case, the object is the Zener card chosen by the sender. Like telepathy, the results of this kind of clairvoyant experiment are unaffected by the distance between the sender and receiver. Clairvoyance appears to operate outside the confines of distance.

Precognition is the ability to predict future events using non-physical senses; it is also called making predictions, foresight, prescience, and/or the regrettable term, "fortune telling". In testing for precognition, time is an important factor. Therefore, there is no sender. Instead, the receiver guesses the correct order of shuffled cards *before the cards are shuffled.* Card decks are then shuffled by an automatic card shuffler or a computer if the deck is computerized. Results indicate that guessing the correct order of the cards is unaffected by the receiver predicting the order of the cards, before the cards are shuffled. Timing does not affect precognition experiment results. Precognition appears to operate outside the confines of time.

Incredibly, on average the statistical results of these telepathy, clairvoyance, and precognition tests were found to be statistically significant. In other words, obtained results averaged well above chance events (Fontana 2010; Rhine, 1937, 1948, 1954).

The implications of the above experimental findings are profound. They suggest that at some level our minds are capable of operating outside of space (distance) and time. Therefore, it is conceivable that when our physical body stops functioning, telepathy, clairvoyance, and precognition become free to function at a fuller capacity. After death, we no longer have a physical body that limits our minds. Therefore, our minds are freed from the confines of space and time (at least as we understand space and time on Earth). In other words, *consciousness continues after the change called death.* In applying the above findings to mediumship, mediums may have developed a strong ability to work outside the limits of space and time. However, because mediums still have a physical body, their abilities probably cannot approach that of a spirit person's.

In the 1970s, the above experiments were upgraded to Ganzfeld tests which incorporate sensory deprivation. The idea is that by reducing sensory inputs like sound and sight (physical sensations), the receiver's mind becomes quiet enough to sense psychic input (non-physical sensations). During a Ganzfeld test, the receiver sits in a room protected from outside distractions while listening to a guided relaxation exercise through headphones and wearing eye goggles. Once the receiver is very relaxed, the sender picks a card or a photo and mentally projects its image to the receiver. Over the years, this experiment has been tweaked many times, bringing it to near perfection against biases, clues, or whatever else might possibly affect results. Like the above telepathy, clairvoyance, and precognition experiments, Ganzfeld experimental results are not affected by distance or time.

A meta-analysis merges data from many experiments on the same phenomena into one big study. The data is then methodically run through rigorous statistical analyses to test for significance. Researchers ran a meta-analysis on Ganzfeld-telepathy experiments conducted from 1970 to 2010. Meta-analysis results indicated odds against chance to be an incredible 13 billion trillion to 1 (Radin, 2013).

Physicists use the term locality to describe the principle that in order for one object to influence another object, they must be spatially close to each other. In addition, a particle traveling through space is limited by the speed of light because it cannot instantaneously influence another particle. Quantum mechanics is the mathematics of matter and light on the atomic or subatomic levels. Quantum mechanics predicts that non-local influences can occur (Greene, 2005). Einstein was so unnerved by this possibility that he called it "spooky action at a distance" (Popkin, 2018, par. 3). The phenomenon of non-locality is well established. It is non-locality that makes it possible for a satellite to communicate with Earth, for the internet to connect globally and for cellphones to communicate with people halfway around the planet. I bring up the concept of non-locality to suggest that perhaps psychic-mediumship will someday be understood through non-locality. After all, the science of psychic phenomena is in its infancy.

Science constantly updates itself on what it considers to be normal. For example, for many centuries, Western civilization believed that everything in the universe revolved around the Earth. To say otherwise was to risk being jailed or even burned at the stake. In addition, if one claimed to be able to see and hear people at great distances, one could be accused of witchcraft. Today, seeing and hearing people in Japan while sitting on one's couch in the United States is called video conferencing. Today, we take for granted that the Earth revolves around the sun as part of a solar system, that there are many solar systems in our galaxy, that our galaxy is one of a vast number of galaxies in our universe, and that there may be multi-universes. Technology like computers, cellphones, teleconferencing, and GPS navigators were once unthinkable but are now common household facts; in modern life, we probably could not live without them. It is the nature of science to progress by pushing the boundaries of what is normal (Sheldrake, 2013).

METHOD

When I type while in a light trance for Linda and Frank, I perceive spirit messages through my seven clairs. Of course, not all seven clairs are simultaneously experienced. However, I often experience two clairs at once; usually clairaudience, clairvoyance, and/or clairempathy. The other four clairs come and go as needed, as determined by my spirit team.

Regarding clairaudience, I hear Linda speaking to me. Sometimes this is experienced thought patterns that form English words as I type. It is as though an intelligence, probably that of my spirit team and Linda's, is translating the thought patterns into words. To me, this feels as if I am hearing with my ears, but not exactly. It reminds me of telepathy in the sense of mind-to-mind. At other times, my clairaudience is similar to hearing during normal, everyday life; I hear specific words, phrases and sentences which have a cadence and a rhythm, just like normal speech. This applies to other sounds as well including music, running water, songs, animals, etc. No matter which way I hear, I perceive it non-physically in my right ear, my head, and my spiritual mind . . . simultaneously. In addition, I toggle back and forth between the two modalities of hearing (i.e., thought patterns and non-physical normal hearing). Both modalities blend into one another so quickly that it is often difficult to discern between the two.

Regarding clairvoyance, I perceive images in my mind. This occurs during pre-session meditations, while typing responses to Frank's questions or mid-session. Visualizations are mostly from Linda but sometimes also from Frank's relatives, Spirit Guide(s), or even my own spirit team. Linda always lets me know when she and I have psychically connected to work; often this happens with an image of her smiling and encouraging me. At other times, I will hear her or sense her presence. On at least one occasion while working on my introduction to this book, Linda appeared to me behind my right shoulder. In addition, I felt her hand on my shoulder as she encouraged me in this work. She was smiling at me in that ever-so-kind-and sweet way of hers.

I often sense clairempathy when working with Linda. This includes emotions that are serious, joyous, soothing, concerned, humorous, annoyed . . . you name it. When reading through the transcripts, it is my hope that readers can discern Linda's breadth of emotions, just as it is with any Earth person. I either feel them clairempathically or they are apparent simply from the words and thoughts she communicates. Linda often uses emotions like joy and humor to communicate with Frank. I really enjoy those moments!

Regarding clairsentience, I experience it both physically and non-physically. An example of physical clairsentience occurs when my hair stands straight up on my head or other body parts. When this happens, it feels like an electric charge running over the surface of my body. The sensation of an electric charge can indicate Linda's presence. However, it can also be my own spirit people, or a combination of Linda and my spirit people. I can simultaneously sense clairsentiently and clairempathically when I feel emotion literally in my physical heart.

Sometimes, non-physical emotional perceptions are so subtle that I cannot describe it as a physical sensation. The emotion occurs in my inner being or knowing. I just know without knowing how and without feeling the emotion. I have to wonder if this is a form of clair-cognition (i.e., simply knowing).

Speaking of claire-cognition . . . claire-cognition occurs when I know something without knowing how I know it. I just know it. This feels like a bright light has suddenly been turned on in my mind. I really experience it like a sudden "aha" moment. Information simply downloads into my conscious awareness and a mystery is solved. There are times when the download is so fast and extensive that I have to remind the spirit people to slow down. I would like to add that Linda has never done that when communicating with me. Even in spirit, her sensitivity to other people is evident.

Although experienced less frequently, sometimes I perceive scents and tastes through clairambience and clairalience. This includes perceiving the scent of flowers, cologne, food, etc. Once while working with Frank, I suddenly sensed the fragrance of a man's cologne. It turns out that Frank has a specific men's cologne he has been wearing for many years and of which Linda would be aware. It was probably a validation to Frank from Linda that she still remembers his favorite scent.

OPENING TO SPIRIT

During the morning of a session, I will open myself up to spirit through a ritual which involves a singing bowl, prayer, and meditation. I begin by playing the singing bowl and reciting my prayer. Incidentally, I wrote this prayer specifically for my work as a medium over a period of two years. Next, I meditate for 30 minutes while listening to spiritual music. I use headphones because they help block out distractive noise.

This ritual is a signal to my spirit people that I am ready to work. In addition, it helps me "get into the zone", where my sensitivities are freer to connect with spirit people. While in the zone, I work with Linda on Frank's questions which have been emailed to me prior to the session. Through mediumship, I type Linda's responses into a transcript for Frank. I know that Linda is always with me when I do this work because I can see, hear, and/or feel her presence with my non-physical senses. After the session, I email Frank the transcript and the recorded audio. When we first started this work in January of 2023, transcribed responses consisted of barely one page. By August 2024 they had increased to six pages.

In addition to inducing a very relaxed mind state, my ritual helps raise my vibrational frequencies. From a spiritualist perspective, we on Earth vibrate on a lower level than do those in the spirit world. The idea is that if we raise our vibrations and spirit people lower theirs, it is easier for our two worlds to connect at that sweet point in between.

I like to think of my altered state of consciousness as just that: an altered state of consciousness. I am always aware of my surroundings, just not as much as during normal waking consciousness. The difference between my waking consciousness and light trance consciousness is very subtle. It requires a very developed sense of mindfulness.

HOW DOES THIS WORK?

You might ask, "Well, I have an idea of how cellphones and the Internet work. It requires cables, satellites, wires, radio waves, and other infrastructure. But how in the world do mediums do this?" Based on my own experiences and from what I have read, heard, and studied, the following is the way I understand how mediumship works.

In order for communication to take place between the two worlds, I blend my auric field with my spirit team and with Frank's aura. This is facilitated by the ritual described above. I mentally picture my aura increasing in size and brightness. I also ask Linda and my guides to come closer to my aura; this is sometimes called auric blending. Linda then works with my spirit people to send psychic information to me. The information is then passed onto Frank either through light trance writing or while speaking with Frank during the phone call. Although Frank is on the West Coast and I am on the East Coast, distance does not matter.

I like to think of mediums as if they are a radio. The medium's body serves as a sensitive antenna that receives messages from the spirit world. Like a radio, a variety of factors help produce very clear communications to not-so-clear communications. From a traditional physics viewpoint, the analogy of a medium being a radio is probably flawed. Nonetheless, many mediums find it useful to describe spirit messages as energies that have a high vibrational frequency.

Like people on Earth, communicating between the two worlds is very important to spirit people. When working with Frank, everyone's spirit team participates. This includes my own spirit team, Frank's, and Linda's. Yes, spirit people can have Spirit Guides! In addition, spirit relatives, loved ones, and friends also like to join the party. From my own experiences with mediumship, when word gets out in the spirit world that someone will be working with a medium, many spirit people want to come to observe the event. From my understanding, large groups of spirit people can help facilitate messages. They can produce greater psychic energy, like an electric generator or a battery. Large amounts of psychic energy help deliver spirit messages and increase the medium's sensitivities.

I like to think of mediumship as a coming together of minds and hearts. A physical body may cease functioning, but the mind and emotions continue to function. In other words, consciousness continues after death.

There are times when I feel as though Linda has connected on her own, without having to work through my spirit people. During such times, I know that my spirit team is with me because they always are. But perhaps, they have just stepped back a bit because Linda is so trustworthy. To me, this shows how well intended and genuine Linda is. It is a pleasure to work with her and Frank. Often, when working with Linda, I sense her gentleness and deep gratitude with my physical heart. Linda's intelligence and ability to communicate cannot be overstated. She is truly a spirit friend to me.

A MESSAGE FROM THE SPIRIT WORLD

As you probably already know, I practice meditation. Sometimes, meditating morphs into a state of moderate trance. This is when spirit may speak through me (i.e., trance speaking). During such times, I become less aware of my surroundings than I am during trance writing; I am in a deeper state of trance. I have little awareness of time and 30 minutes feels like five minutes. Such states end easily and gently, usually right before the timer goes off. I am always in complete control of everything.

Sometimes my speaking in trance is audio-recorded. Below is an excerpt from such an occasion. I believe the speaker is one of my main Spirit Guides. This transcription was edited to be reader-friendly, and the end quote was added post-edit.

This morning, spirit would like to talk about the practice of sharing our light, in the form of mediumship, in order to better the world. This is something which all people should be doing to a lesser or greater degree. For mediumship is as much a part of nature as is the weather, the night sky, all creatures swimming, walking, or flying upon the Earth. It is as normal as being born and breathing the air we breathe. It is a wonderful way to bring hope and solace to a world in dire need. What we are talking about is the willingness to attest that communing with loved ones and guides in spirit, is not only possible, but it is a normal part of life. It is part of the natural world and not something to fear or avoid.

From our perspective, the main purpose of mediumship is to demonstrate that life continues after the transition called death. Consciousness was with us before we were born, is with us now and will continue long after our physical bodies have ceased functioning. And whether such demonstrations of mediumship are for oneself or for the sake of others, whether they are in small or great measure, it does not matter. What matters is that there is the intent to commune with spirit, to bring messages from us in spirit to those on Earth, for we are all part of a greater whole. We are not as divided into the physical world versus the non-physical worlds as we are generally taught to believe.

All of our thoughts count, small and big thoughts, all have meanings beyond mere utterances. For thoughts are actual things and are not to be trifled with. In a sense, thoughts are a kind of energy. And as increasingly more thought-energies agree that truth in life is far more spiritual than it is material, at some point a critical point is reached in the ethers. This critical point represents a realization for increasing numbers of people that spirit communication is a normal part of the Earth experience. This is not a belief, it is a knowing, just as gnosis is knowing through experience.

Just as spouses often know one another's thoughts without a word being spoken, thought-energies can, and are, transmitted about us non-physically. This is commonly known as telepathy but goes by other names as well. Some thought-energies can accumulate in energy and power as they become increasingly more common. For example, as increasingly more people understand that spirit communication is real, such thought-energies to that effect accrue in our psychic atmosphere. Eventually, a critical point in understanding is reached that spirit communication is real and a fact, thereby becoming a defining outlook of our culture. Just as the concept that the Earth rotates around the sun is now taken for granted, so will the concept of life after death become part and parcel of our culture once that critical point is reached through thought-energies. We are fast approaching this juncture.

It is important that we all play our role in this great awakening. We must not allow fear to discourage us from our own practices of mediumship, in whatever form it may take. It doesn't matter if you do readings, support those who do readings, if you commune with spirit through nature, if you meditate, practice automatic writing, or if you look for signs from spirit . . . don't be shy about speaking up! Push back against the naysayers who try to discourage us every chance they get.

The more that spirit communication is normalized and understood, the less suffering people will experience when it becomes their time to transition. This is true for those about to transition as well as their loved ones who will be remaining on Earth a while longer. It is imperative that your culture changes in its understanding of the Afterlife.

For it is in the knowing that there is life after death, that peace will be brought to people, a peace that unfortunately, most people never get to experience. And so, it is your responsibility to demonstrate in small or great measure, the existence, the reality, that consciousness continues after the change called death. It is not a maybe, it is not a belief, it's a fact. For consciousness was there before you were born, it is with you during life, it will be there when your physical body ceases. We ask all people to constantly practice your mediumship and psychic abilities, whether in small or great measure, by yourself and/or with others. Take what abilities you have, no matter how small or big, and build upon it. Let's all help accumulate thought-energies in the ethers to such an extent that it will reach that critical point that changes our world from one that focuses on materialism to one that is deeply aware of our non-physical, spiritual nature.

There is much in the media and other sources that paint an erroneous picture of what spirit communication is like. On the one hand, religion may paint mediumship as demonic while medicine views it is a form of mental illness. Fortunately, such misinformed opinions are slowly changing.

Mainstream science still insists that consciousness is a product of the physical body. Many scientists believe consciousness to be the result of a random set of chemicals that by chance happened to develop the physical world. However, many other scientists are beginning to challenge this assumption. To quote:

Most scientists believe that consciousness came after life, as a product of evolution. But observations of extraterrestrial organic material, along with Roger Penrose and Stuart Hameroff's quantum theory of consciousness, provide reason to believe that consciousness came before life. In fact, argue Hameroff and his collaborators, consciousness may have been what made evolution and life possible in the first place. (Hameroff, Bandyopadhyay, and Dante, 2024, p. 1)

BIBLIOGRAPHY

Edwards, Harry. 2003. *A Guide for the Development of Mediumship*. Middlesex, UK: Con-Psy Publications.

Fontana, David. 2010. *Is There an Afterlife?* Winchester, UK: O Books.

Greene, Brian, PhD. 2005. *The Fabric of the Cosmos. Vintage Books*: United States of America.

Hameroff, Stuart, Anirban Bandyopadhyay, and Lauretta Dante. "Consciousness Came before Life." *IAI News*, (2024). Accessed May 8, 2024. /articles/life-and-consciousness-what-are-they-auid-2836.

Klimo, Jon. 1987. *Channeling: Investigations on Receiving Information from Paranormal Sources. Jeremy P. Tarcher, Inc.*: Los Angeles.

McVaugh, Michael R. 2006. "Rhine Research Center." NCPedia. Encyclopedia of North Carolina, https://www.ncpedia.org/rhine-research-center.

Moustakas, C. 1994. *Phenomenological Research Methods*. Sage Publication Inc.: Thousand Oaks, CA.

Myers, Frederic C. 1906. *Human Personality and Its Survival of Bodily Death*. Create Space Independent Publishing Platform 2016. 1535542624.

Popkin, Gabriel. "Einstein's 'Spooky Action at a Distance' Spotted in Objects Almost Big Enough to See." *Science*, (2018). https://doi.org/doi.org/10.1126/science.aat9920.

Radin, Dean PhD. 2013. *Supernormal. Crown Publishing Book*: New York.

Rhine, J.B. 1937. *New Frontiers of the Afterlife*. New York: Farrar & Rinehart.

Rhine, J.B. 1948. *The Reach of the Mind. Faber & Faber*: London.

Rhine, J.B. 1954. *New World of the Mind. Faber & Faber*: London.

Sheldrake, Rupert. 2013. *The Sense of Being Stared At. Park Street Press*: Rochester, Vermont.

Wahbeh, Helena, Kelly McDermott, and Amira Saghar. "Dissociative Symptoms and Anomalous Information Reception." *Activitas Nervosa Superior 60*, (2018). https://doi.org/doi.org/10.1007/s41470-018-0023-6.

COMMUNICATION SESSIONS

INTRODUCTORY TO COMMUNICATION SESSIONS

What follows, Dear Reader, is a list of transactions between our medium, Elizabeth Raver, Ph.D., who is in her office; Linda, who is in the Afterlife; and Frank, who is at home. Frank and Liz are connected by phone, as they live on opposite coasts. Liz sends to Frank, after each mediumship session, an audio recording and a written transcript of the entire conversation. You will be able to read all of them.

01/29/2023

F TO E:
Thanks so much for your email of explanations. I am fine with Zoom. I will check out your reading list. FYI: I have read 14 books in nine weeks on this science/art/technology mainly because I couldn't sleep, and I'm a fast reader, and my wife is paramount in my life. I continue to read books about this amazing science, and to learn how to communicate with her. She was/is wonderful and really loves me. I started my reading with the quantum mechanics folks, then the scientists, psychologists, scholars, and on to the practitioners. I've read R. Craig Hogan, Gary Schwartz, Ph.D., et al. A fascinating group of researchers. Now I need to learn how to communicate with Linda, which I know she wants. I look forward to our session, Elizabeth. Thank you.

Frank

E COMMENTS:
As mentioned in the introduction, Frank is an avid reader. This is one of the things that made me notice how sincere he is in wanting to learn how to connect with Linda. And that he is highly intelligent. I especially appreciated that he is not afraid to delve into quantum mechanics as it may pertain to mediumship.

The above document is the only one we kept when we first started working. As we move on in time, it will be clear that the documents morph into much more than mere emails exchanges.

We quickly ended up having sessions via telephone conversations, not Zoom.

02/09/2023

E TO F:

I enjoyed working with you today during your session. I hope you are doing well. Linda is beautiful . . . it was such a pleasure to "meet" her today.

On another note, I am glad you wrote that the session was "great". I really enjoyed working with you and Linda! You two *still* make a great team, full of much love.

03/09/2023

E:
Hello Frank,

Thank you for the lovely and productive session today! You are awesome. This is not just me saying this, but spirit itself said to me, during your session that you are doing remarkably well, better than most people, especially under the circumstances (having been married for so long to someone you loved so much and who loved you back so much).

Here is the channeled message from Linda obtained while I was meditating before our session:

I (Elizabeth) am playing music while meditating before our phone call. Through the music itself, Linda communicates to me that the music is about "a great love" (meaning a great love between you and her). Then her words are as follows:

L:
I have never left you, my love. I'm here for you now and forever. We're meant to journey together on the boat of life. Please understand how much I care about you. And miss you. But time has no value over here, so for me you'll be with me again sooner than you can blink.

I'll always be at your side, my love, my love. It's all part of life's mysteries, this ebb and flow of birth, death, rebirth, and so on. The life cycle continues after the "shell" ceases. I'm really with you my love, in mind and heart. I'm there. I'm waiting . . . but only when the time is right and not an Earth-minute before. But I'm still with you NOW, with or without a medium!

F COMMENTS:
This was my second session with Elizabeth and Linda. The first one was not recorded. Here you can see that Linda is able to give free expression to her feelings, and we were able to have a short conversation; my part is absent due to a technical difficulty.

Reader, please remember that Linda is an artist—poetry, performance art, music, and film. She is a "word master".

E COMMENTS:

This communication occurred during the initial stages of my working with Frank and Linda. Interestingly, Linda used the music I was meditating with to communicate with me. I believe I was being given a portent of what was to come, in terms of sessions with Frank and Linda. Spirit people often view mediumship sessions as communication experiments. In addition, I believe that Linda was already working with other spirit people. The intent was/is to develop a communication method for Linda and Frank, using me as the intermediary psychic-medium. I feel that spirit hopes that other mediums, sitters, and belated loved ones could follow suit; perhaps they could even build on it this work.

    As sessions proceeded over time they became longer, more detailed, and, most of all, more conversational. To me, mediumship development never ends as there is always something more to learn and experience.

03/14/2023

F TO E:
Hi Elizabeth,

I just reread your notes in blue and the message Linda had for me—sweet, touching, I am a lucky man, she is so wonderful!

Yes, I like Fontana's book a lot. And I just bought *Beyond Biocentrism* by Bob Berman and Robert Lanza; among other topics, a study into the evolution into the modern world of the study of the Afterlife and consciousness.

I am very busy the next couple of weeks, but I would like to schedule another reading with you and my Linda maybe late March/early April.

Thanks for your note and take care.

Frank

E COMMENTS:
At this time in our session, we were meeting once a month. By the end of 2023, this changed to two or even three times per month. During the slower period of time, I believe we were slowly building up energetic momentum with the spirit world. This buildup was slow in the beginning so that Frank, Linda and I had plenty of time to become accustomed to the way we would be working. It is a matter of quality, not quantity.

04/10/2023

F:
Did you tell me that Linda said she had met my parents?

E:
Yes, as I recall I saw them together in addition to "feeling impressed" that they had connected in the spirit world. Also, if my memory serves me correctly, that your parents were some of the spirit people who helped Linda to transition.

F:
She met Mom a few times when they were both alive. She never met Dad, as he died just a few months before I met her. I have always wished she had met Dad. He thought poetry is the highest form of art; Linda is a poet. Well, she has met him since then, albeit in spirit! Since they are both wonderful poets, I am sure they are continuing their poetic work in the Afterlife.

E COMMENTS:
As our communication methodology was still in its primary stages, the April 2023 transcript is not particularly complex. All sessions with Frank on the phone are an hour long (not including my pre-session preparations). This transcription is but a fraction of what took place on April 10, 2023. Nonetheless, it is a good idea to include it so the reader can observe transcripts morphing over time.

05/01/2023

F TO E:
WOW!! Wonderful—I can hardly believe it!

    I appreciate so much that you communicated with her. Very interesting.

    I am sorry I don't know the protocols for everything yet, so you do the meeting however you want on Thursday. I love her very much, and she does me, which makes it painful for me to not have her here. This is why I want to learn more about this science. BTW: Just finished my 24th book really a good one—*Love and the Afterlife* by Julie Beischel, Ph.D.

F:
Have you met my mom and dad?

L:
You know I have. We are together, among many others, through familial relations, friendly relations, both knowing those when I was on the planet with you, and not knowing personally but knowing about. Your parents are very wonderful to me. They and others are helping me to adjust. Oh Frank, you have no idea just how beautiful this place is. I look forward to when you join us . . . but only when it is your time. Not a minute before, not a second before. You still have many things to accomplish while you are an incarnate. Everything was prepared for me before I arrived, and your parents were part of that project. Every need is taken care of here, every thought heard, every deed counted, every heart heard. There is no hiding. It is beautiful. The colors are indescribable. Don't worry about me, Frank, I am doing unbelievably well. It is so joyous here. You mustn't hurt so much, for it hurts my heart to know your heart is heavy. You are doing very well, better than you know, since I have left my body. I am surrounded by love. So are you . . . there is just this physical barrier that makes it difficult for you to perceive us.

    This physical barrier, the human body, is what keeps those in a physical body from sensing us. That is the way it is supposed to be. Your body and emotions and mind all work in tandem; when your mind and emotions are focused on grief, or even work, then it becomes more difficult for us to connect in a way you are consciously aware of. You can't just "wish" it or force it or even study it to make it happen. Just be as you are, finding joy in everything you do from mundane to not so mundane tasks. Let your mind free flow and there I will be.

F:
Do you know I met with Quentin Ring on Friday, April 21st, about the Linda book I did, and the Linda J. Albertano scholarship I will create?

L:
I do know about these things because I make it a point to know what my Frank is up to. (**E:** I hear Linda laugh.) *I am working with you on the scholarship . . . even if you cannot sense me, I am there, helping you in your unconscious mind. I am so happy that you are doing this to help others (the scholarship). Frank, if you talk to yourself and it feels like I am answering back in your mind, this is not your imagination. It really is me. You won't hear me like you did when I was on Earth. It is much subtler than that. It is like a daydream or imagination. Except that it is really me. Free flow your mind in conversations with me, my love.*

F:
Were you at the meeting?

L:
Yes, Frank, I was there. My love, I was there. Just be as you are . . . I am there whether or not you are aware of me. So are others in spirit with you. I am helping you, but others are too . . . your parents are some of those helping. They are better at this sort of thing than I am as they have been in spirit for a longer time than I have. I still have much to learn so am sometimes limited in what I can communicate. But they and others are helping us.

E COMMENTS:
In this transcript, Frank mentions that he has a book written by Julie Beischel, PhD. Dr. Beischel is a well-known and accomplished consciousness researcher, especially as it pertains to mediumship and other kinds of after death communications. She is the Director of Research at the Windbridge Research Center, located in Arizona. Her work and publications are worth reading as she is truly a pioneer in this field.

05/04/2023

L:

Frank, my love, my dear, I'm here waiting for you. You don't need to do this, to always need to know if I am aware of what's happening on the planet; for I am always in your heart and mind. I'm very much aware of all that goes on in your life because of the strong bonds formed while we were together on Earth. I am aware of what goes on with you and our friends. I am certainly aware of activities occurring that are related to me. It is much easier for me to be aware of what is going on in Earth, than it is for Earth people to be aware of what happens in the spiritual realms. It has been designed to be that way.

I haven't been here all that long, so I haven't yet had the need to completely un-attach myself to my emotional and physical love bonds of Earth . . . with you being on the top of the list! At some point, however, in the future, I will naturally have weaker connections with my Earthly bonds, as I grow in spirit, in heaven.

This is not to say that we won't be able to communicate. Quite the contrary. Because you also, even while on Earth, are also slowly, oh so slowly, letting go of Earthly attachments. The less Earthly attachments one has, the finer and subtler will be your mind and heart; and this will help facilitate communication between us.

You can't force this or wish this into being, any more than one can force a flower to bloom whilst it is barely growing out of the soil as a stem. It won't work because of the natural laws pertaining to heaven and Earth. Especially the natural Law of Rhythm. Everything must be in the exact correct position of location, time and consciousness for any given event to occur. This also applies to the non-material worlds, spiritual; even though it is said that time doesn't exist on the other side, it is more accurate to say that over here, in the Afterlife, time is so different, that for all practical purposes we may as well say to people on Earth that time doesn't exist, when in fact time does exist in the Afterlife.

I'm so excited about your therapy session and there I will most certainly be! I wouldn't miss it for the world! What strange worlds we both live in, having to communicate like this.

E NOTE:

Linda channeled the above message before Frank's session. In addition to Linda's message, Frank's parents also came through. His mom came through the strongest, as I felt her warmth and kindness very energetically in my heart. I saw his mom and Linda standing next to each other; Frank's mom had her arm around Linda even though his mom is shorter than her. It was a funny moment. Both were happy and smiling. I was told that Frank's dad is helping Linda with her communications to Frank.

E COMMENTS:

The above "E note" was added onto the original transcript after Frank's session. It was not included in the original transcript because I was still learning to incorporate pre-session experiences into the transcripts. Eventually, I figured out how to do this in a reader-friendly manner.

05/24/2023

F:
Did you see me getting therapy last week?

L:
Why ask me such a question when you know my love, that I would never leave you. I have every reason to want to be part of your therapy sessions, especially knowing that you are doing this in order to connect with me. Our bond is so strong emotionally and mentally how could I not, as your intent for our love to continue on is great. The mere lack of my physical body cannot stop that.

E TO F:
During our session, while I was reading this to you, Frank, Linda impressed upon me that she too is dealing with emotional issues and that may also be playing a role in how well she can communicate with you and/or how well you can sense her communication attempts. After all, she has not been on the other side for a long time, at least not yet. There is much for her to become accustomed to, to learn, to adapt to, in addition to learning how to communicate with you.

L:
More importantly, instead of asking if I was there, it is I that should be asking you if you sensed me there, for surely I was there indeed. If not in body, then certainly with my mind and heart. Absolutely, I was there. I felt that you could sense me but also that you were simply doubting yourself, having been using your rational mind for so, so many years and not used to this new way of perceiving. I, too, am "struggling" to sense without my physical body. They tell me it takes practice and time (**E:** By Earth's standards.)

They (spirit) work on me too, while you are having EMDR sessions. In order for us to better connect, we both need to work on our own personalities, healings, distractions, attachments (letting go of them), to better connect.

F:
Have we been able to communicate directly lately? I think so, a few times. This past Saturday seemed like a good connection, we talked for a little while.

L:
Yes, yes, yes! We have been. It is not your imagination. You have no idea how happy this makes me. Not only that, but also your parents and others, including guides, rejoice when we . . . any one of us, not just myself . . . communicate with you and you sense and perceive us. It is cause for celebration.

F:
Question from Alexandra: Do you have any message for her, how she should proceed with her life?

L:
This is a heavy question that is being asked of me and I can no more respond correctly than if I were still on Earth. I have not gained instant wisdom, all seeing, simply because I am without a body . . .
   To Alexandra: "Go ahead with your plans . . . we learn and gain by doing. It is the experience of doing that matters from our vantage point."

E TO F:
It is very difficult to respond to a third-party inquiry like this. Many factors involved in receiving a good reading.

F:
I love you very much, always will, am very proud of you, and I'm very proud of our long, loving relationship.

L:
And I love you too, very much, my love and always will. I am also proud of you, doing so much on my behalf since my passing but also standing on your lonesome and still accomplishing so much. We have much in common and continue to have much in common, it's just that now I do not have a physical body as you knew it when I was on Earth.

F:

Elizabeth, FYI: Last Saturday, I asked Linda, "Does it rain there?" She said, *"It just seems to get wet, then dries up."* Does that sound right?

Also, I asked her about healing, she said it was a lot of psychological healing . . .

E TO F:

(This has been paraphrased and is not verbatim.) I have heard various reports describing how water behaves on the other side. One can walk into a lake with clothes on after which, when one walks out of the lake, the water just rolls over/off the body/clothes. The water does not "stick" so to speak, and the body/clothes are instantly dry. In addition, Linda's reference to water may have had a dual meaning because water can also represent emotion. So, she may also be referring to her dealing with emotions . . . I have no way of being able to verify either of these possibilities.

E COMMENTS:

It is now towards the end of May 2023. The question-and-answer process is beginning to morph into something more conversational. Transcripts are also becoming longer.

F COMMENTS:

Yes, as the communication between Linda and me became better, more facile, the Reading sessions got better, as you can see.

06/23/2023

E TO F:
During a short meditation, even before I rang my Tibetan bowl and said my prayer, this came through:

I felt the strong presence of Linda's father. I heard *"Can I speak with you?"* To which I mentally replied that it was up to Frank, not me. Then I felt Linda's presence and was impressed with the strong sense that Linda was here with her father. I wrote the following:

L:
I have met with my father and sorted things out about my past. It's all positive and good and helping me to let go of attachments to "ancient" negativities from some of my experiences while on Earth. It's amazing how this works . . . the basis of all this is love, which is what carries us forth into our new worlds. You will see, my love, when your turn comes. I love you so much and miss you, but I am learning how to make myself "better perceived" by you, everyday (though we don't have the same sense of time here as you have on Earth). It is all part of the grand plan, the grand scheme of life. We come into Earth, we are born into the Earth, and then when the time comes, we are born out of Earth, we are born into the other worlds (heaven). So it is . . .

I will always be there for you Frank, all you need do is think of me, put out an intent that I am there, with you; or say a prayer that I am there; or mentally think of me or write down on paper that you want me there . . . and there, I will be there.

I am frequently there with you, whether or not you request my presence. This is because of my love for you. Actually, I am there a LOT more than you realize. But then again, I do have my activities in the other realms. These other activities are very important for my adjustment and growth in this new world. Still, you just request me, or put out an intention for me, or a prayer that I be there . . . and I will be there. Just like the James Taylor song: "just call out my name, and you know wherever I am, I will be there, yes I will . . . " I don't yet understand how this works, but it does indeed work. And it has been going on for ages, people of Earth communicating with their loved ones in spirit. Oh, mysteries of mysteries!

F TO E:
FYI: I had a clairvoyant vision of Linda today, I think—and I saw her standing in a kitchen, I think . . .

E TO F:
This is very good progress! Most people wait years to visually see a loved one who has passed; if indeed, they ever do. Just now, as I type this, Lynda wants you to know how proud and excited and happy she is that you were able to see her. She is calling it a milestone.

F:
I had no idea they have kitchens in the Afterlife! I didn't think they eat! But—what do I know . . . nothing!

E TO F:
Linda just corrected me, regarding how to spell her name. It is Linda with an "i", not a "y".

I will answer this question based on how I understand this. In the Afterlife they have whatever they need to feel comfortable. So, if Linda needs an apartment with curtains, that will indeed appear. In addition, spirit people will often appear to us in ways we can relate. Appearing to you in a kitchen is a great way to present herself. However, I think in this case the kitchen is symbolizing something. We can talk about this on the phone in more depth. It is not so much that they have kitchens in the Afterlife, as it is Linda using the symbol of a kitchen. Maybe she liked to cook, maybe you need to cook more food and pay more attention to what you are eating, maybe she feels a kitchen scene brings a sense of comfort . . .

F TO E:
Actually Elizabeth, I feel sort of like a fish out of water with some of my questions—I'm not sure how appropriate they are, given her present circumstances. I would really like to ask her how she is feeling, but I don't know how emotional it is for her to deal with that question. She is there due to pancreatic cancer, which ended her life early. She was very productive and mentally active up to the end, with a lot more that she wanted to do.

Can she, Linda, hear me when I am riding on my bicycle or in my car driving, and talking to her (which I do out loud in both cases)? Or in my living room?

L:
Yes to all of the above, Frankie! At some point, you won't even need to do it out loud but within your mind, mentally . . .

F:
Does she know that Taj Mahal is going to write a testimonial about her for the big book of photos and poems I am doing about her?

L:
Of course!

F:
Taj called me a few days ago, loves Linda. (Liz, Taj Mahal is one of the most famous and popular Blues musicians in the world during the past 50 years.)

E:
(As I read this question, I feel Linda close to me and I see her opening her eyes, in gratitude. She then takes a deep breath and says, *"This will keep Frankie busy and happy,"* and sort of laughs. I feel her love for you in my heart . . .)

F:
Are you writing? If so, with what—pen/pencil, or computer, or what?

E:
I have no way of validating this question. Linda shows me herself writing with her mind. It is as if the intent of her thoughts, come out from her pre-frontal cortex and onto paper . . . *"spirit paper"* I hear her say and *"I love doing this, it is so much fun."* (*"Yes,"* she says to me in response to what I had just written.)

F:
Where do you get your clothes?

L:
They just are. I wear what I feel most comfortable in, I just think them and there they are. Actually, I don't even think of what clothes to wear, they are just there. Very similar to what I wore on Earth. I think my unconscious is doing the walking for me, when it comes to clothes.

E:
(I hear Linda laugh; I think Linda means that it is her unconscious that creates what she wears. I should add that the longer they are over there, at some point, they just start wearing spirit clothes which essentially look like robes. But when they visit us, they wear the same kind of clothes they wore on Earth so we can recognize them.)

F:
If you want to travel, how do you go—by car, horse and wagon, or how?

L:
(**E:** I hear Linda laugh.) *No horse and wagon unless I want to time travel. We have spirit vehicles we can travel in, but we can also think of where we want to go and end up there. But that takes practice, and most people can't do it for a while after they have arrived.*

F:
Do you know I will love you forever?

L:
And I love you!

E COMMENTS:

On 6/23/2023, it reads:

"Most people wait years to visually see a loved one who has passed; if indeed, they ever do."

My response to Frank's comment about seeing Linda in the kitchen was not entirely accurate. There have been numerous surveys over the years regarding after death visual experiences. However, many still believe this is a taboo topic. This unfortunate belief makes it difficult to estimate how long it takes on average for a griever to clairvoyantly see their late loved one. Based on my own experiences, Frank's abilities are developing unusually quickly. This is most likely due to his commitment, intelligence, sincerity, and open-mindedness.

F COMMENTS:

My first clairvoyant event with Linda—seeing her in situ and seeing her move around while we were talking was truly wonderful! A dream come true for me!

07/27/2023

F:
Linda, I will love you forever, and I never want to be separated from you again! I am so grateful to have you in my life—you are the most wonderful person I know!!

L:
I love you too, Frankie . . . You know this as I have loved you already for a very long time. Love is not lost, nor does it change just because a physical body ceases. Love intensifies, though that is hard to explain. It is like we only have so much energy when on Earth . . . part goes to the body, part to the mind, and part to emotions. When the body ceases, even more energy goes to the mind and to the emotions. Our new bodies are less dense, more subtle. Love and thought, both part of consciousness, continue. I will always be there for you.

F:
Gary and Cydney Mandel send you their love. They know we talk. They were wonderful to me.

L:
I love Gary and Cydney, they are such good people. Tell them I love them too and not to worry! It is all indeed proceeding the way it is meant to. It is all part of the great life cycle. Thank them for supporting and helping you. But they should not worry as there are more unseen beautiful things than meets the naked eye. (**E:** I think she means physical eyesight.)

F:
Are you able to get my questions when we talk? For instance, Scott and I want to find, in your archives, a video tape within the past 20 years, where you are visibly presenting your poetry. Any ideas?

F NOTE:
Linda said "shelves"; Elizabeth had a mental vision "in studio, sit and meditate." I found stuff in both places.

L:
Yes, of course. Love and thought make this possible. Our minds and hearts are connected psychically. However, when I reply to you it is sometimes difficult for you to hear me. Actually, you do perceive me but on an unconscious level. Try looking for different kinds of signs, not necessarily seeing or hearing me. I will do my best to try different ways of connecting. You know, Frankie, flickering lights, butterflies, and other things in nature, objects in odd places, etc. It is all a matter of subtlety.

F:
I spoke with Taj Mahal again. He and Pam Polland are touring, and in every venue are singing "2:10 Train" in your honor. It is one of their favorite songs.

L:
This is like a prayer to me. It helps me to connect with those on Earth. The music's vibrations are akin to my own. It is quite a thrill for me to experience this; it is actually a comfort knowing that I can easily connect with them and the audience even if they are not consciously aware of my presence. It is hilarious, too, at times . . . them singing, me being attracted to the crowd, but them not seeing me, but they keep on singing. We think this is hilarious on our side. Jokes abound about such as "what, why can't they see me?"

F:
Are you able to read or see any of my recent poems about you and me, like "The Missing . . . " and "Who Was She?"?

L:
(**E:** I hear Linda laugh.) *I don't need to read it anymore, like people on Earth do. I can sense it, sense the words through your aura. You can't hide anything from me anymore. These two poems are poignant, and I just want to reach out and literally scream, "Frank, I am HERE. Right now! I never left, it was just that old body of mine that was worn out. But ME, LINDA, lives on in a way that is even MORE full of life than when I had to wear that physical body, which was like a wet coat to me. It was such a relief to get rid of it. Now the real fun starts in my new life."*

F:
Thanks so much for the wonderful books on Italy that you were saving to give me at some point! We found them in your studio.

L:
You think that if you go to Italy, I won't be there with you. But I will be! Do this for yourself. You still have things to do on Earth, Frank. What's more, I will enjoy helping you to do those things. Actually, there is a group of us here in spirit that are helping you now in all you do; that carries over to any trips you take, any projects . . . even if they don't focus on your wife, Linda.

F:
When is your next performance or show there, where you are? Is it a large venue, like an auditorium, or what?

L:
It's hard to explain. For one thing, I attend shows on Earth that are done in my honor. As for shows in "Summerland" . . . they are not as frequent as when I was on Earth. I am still trying to adjust to the new physics and my new body, new friends here. I do get tired if I do too much. I also am interested in other activities as well. This includes helping people over here when I can. They have choruses here where the most beautiful music is played and the most beautiful voices are heard. I am hoping to participate as a singer at some point. Completely different than music on Earth. By the way, I have been able to connect with some of my friends from Africa who are musicians. Bet you didn't expect to hear that! So learning, experiences and growth continue even more.

F:
Are you having fun? I miss you terribly.

L:
I miss you too, Frankie . . . but you too will be here when the time is right. Short time for me but long time for you as Earth's sense of time is different. As for fun, "joy" might be a more accurate word. When one looks up at the night sky there is a sense of awe and joy. That is what it is like but almost all the time!

F TO E:
Last question—this one for you, Liz:
 Do any of the DLOs ask to speak with their specific Earth-bound relatives or loved ones?

E:
Sometimes.

F TO E:
That's it, Liz—and I hope it's not too much. It's just that sometimes I am not sure how much I am getting through to her, for example, I have asked her about the video in question #3.

F COMMENTS:
So, Dear Reader, you can see that it gets to be more and more fun!

08/17/2023

F:
(Just as session is starting.) I would like to talk with Linda about a few items on Thursday that I hope she will like, and that I hope are not too emotional for her.

L:
Emotions like joy, happiness, love, etc. do not lower my vibrations so there is nothing to worry about. The items you describe only bring joy and love to me.

Emotions are a different experience here in spirit. Unlike Earth, here in spirit we cannot hide our emotions from others or ourselves. Our bodies are made from finer material, and others can see our emotions and read our thoughts. Therefore, when I become emotional it is immediately apparent to others and myself. This inspires me to constantly maintain higher emotions/thoughts.

F:
On Saturday, September 9th, in the afternoon, Beyond Baroque (the famous poetry venue near us) is going to honor Linda, by making the announcement about the fellowship I am creating in her name. It will be called the Linda J. Albertano Fellowship for Women Poets, and I will fund it. Each year, one or two qualified women poets of any age will receive a financial gift to use for poetry writing courses at Beyond Baroque. I will introduce the fellowship to the public.

L:
Frank. this is wonderful. I will do all I can from my side here in spirit to help those who receive the fellowship. I will also do what I can to "tweak" things on Earth so that the right women poets receive the fellowship. This is not for my own self for in spirit we are encouraged to place others before ourselves. This is for poetry itself and for those women who selflessly dedicate themselves to its pursuit. You are giving me an opportunity to help those on Earth who aspire to poetry.

F:
On Sunday, September 17th, at Sheila Pinkel's home, Prince Diabate will be there with his Kora, to play music for the guests, and to raise money for his school in West Africa. He will play and sing the song he has written about Linda and how we all love her. He has named part of his school in Africa after Linda.

L:
I will be there with signs. As with most signs from spirit, they are subtle. If someone thinks they feel my presence but is not sure if it is their imagination, it is not their imagination. I wouldn't miss this for the world! I want people to know that life goes on and it is beautiful here, that I am fine and doing well. Very healthy now. You may feel me in your heart! It won't be your imagination. I am very excited about this. I wouldn't miss this for anything! I will simply "think it" to be there, and there I will be with you all.

F:
I know that I tend to "blab" a lot when I contact her to talk with her. I would like to know what she would like to talk about when I call her.

L:
Frankie, you are so funny. You always "blab" and that is OK with me. It gets the conversation starting. Maybe at some point we could talk about projects or activities that are FOR YOU, not me! You keep giving, giving, giving to me, but when are you going to start thinking of your own activities, things that YOU want to do. It is time, Frankie . . . you can't keep going on with me always in mind. This is difficult for me to say to you. I have trouble finding the right words. But one thing that would make me so happy is if you started doing your own things! Just like on Earth, I will be there with you. But the focus is on you . . . please darling, start doing for you, if only to please me!

F:
I have received the most wonderful, complimentary, and loving tributes to Linda from so many of her friends for the book I have written about her, that we are working to publish: Kat and Peter, Suzanne, Laurel Ann, Prince Diabate, Taj Mahal, Anna Homler, and others.

L:
So long as it brings happiness and joy to others, so long as it inspires others, I am in for this. Earth life is tough enough, as you and I well know. Anything that helps others to feel inspired, be lifted up, to give them hope, that is what is important. I appreciate everyone's efforts but please remember, it is about spreading love and kindness to others to help them on their journey on Earth.

F:
To Linda: I want you to know how much I love you and miss you every minute of every day. We had a wonderful life together for so many years, and it will continue when I arrive and help you with new projects.

L:
Yes, Frank. I love you too my love. You are such a special man and are so special to me. I will always appreciate the things you have done to lift me up in life and the love we shared. You made it possible for me to blossom as a human being, to reach my potential. When you arrive here, (which won't be for some time), I will be first in line to show you around! I will be there to help you cross over. I will be there to show you how wonderful this place is and to settle in, to show you the wonders and how amazing it is. I can't wait 'til we attend our first musical concert as the music experience is so different from Earth's. It is hard to describe until you experience it. This is partly because your new body will be of a finer substance. In the meantime, keep busy with your projects but also start thinking about things YOU want to do. For you still have things to accomplish on Earth . . . I will be with you all the way. For now, my love . . .

09/12/2023

E NOTE:
Communication day before Frank's phone call, September 12th, 2023.

F TO E:
I'm glad you could see some photos of our tribute to my dear Linda at Beyond Baroque, the great poetry venue here in Venice, on this past Saturday, September 9th. She was prominent there for about 50 years and loved the place, as they loved her.

E:
I really enjoyed them, especially the videos. I didn't watch every single video, but my intent is to go back and do so, as soon as I get a chance.

F:
Moving on with my life to me means moving on with you. You are the most important person in my life, always will be. I will love you forever and am lonely without you.

L:
My dear Frank, it is through love and thought that we are able to commune between two different worlds. Our love is so great that to not be able to commune with one another is unthinkable. The laws of cause and effect, when combined with our everlasting and deep affection for each other, is what makes it so possible to continue our love relationship in spite of the fact that one of us does no longer live on Earth. Love is the strongest thing there is in life as it comes from source, the light. Thought is an actual thing and although it is difficult to perceive thought as a thing while one is encased in a physical body, I assure you it is real. My love carries my thoughts to you, and your love carries your thoughts to me.

F:
Our two tributes to you at Beyond Baroque were this past Thursday, and again this past Saturday. I think you were there, and saw the wonderful video Kat (cat) and Peter did of you, plus other videos we showed.

L:
Of course, I saw Kat and Peter's video of me! I would not miss that.

F:
Did you send the hummingbird that flew around Prince Diabate when he sang the song about you on Saturday?

L:
Yes, I did see the hummingbird ... and yes, that was a sign from heaven regarding me. I got help from others in heaven, those who are more experienced in doing such things. It takes a while by Earth standards to learn some things. But yes, the hummingbird was intended as a validation for you, Prince, and everyone attending on Saturday that my consciousness was indeed present. Isn't it wonderful, Frankie! You don't know how happy it makes me feel when such things are done on my behalf. I giggle a bit, it makes me giddy. My Frankie did this for me ...

F:
Will you be at Sheila's home this coming Sunday evening for the benefit for Prince? He is going to sing your song there, too. He cries when he sings it. So do I.

L:
Of course, I will be. I wish people would not cry on my behalf though. Things are wonderful where I am. I am with your parents and others as well. In some ways, it is like Earth and in other ways it is completely different. People are so much kinder to one another. We don't have the heaviness that accompanies Earth experiences, that density caused by our bodies and the atmosphere

and environment on Earth. We are free!!! But it pains us to see our loved ones on Earth suffer on our behalf. We have everything we need here, love. Nothing wants. And we are surrounded by love and light and all the corny stuff which turns out to be not so corny once one arrives and experiences it. So please sing, sing, sing "my" song but sing it with joy, happiness, gratitude, and peace.

F:
Alex and I have found some old VHS and film of you and are trying to get it transferred to digital to show people about you via computer projection.

L:
So, you found them?! Ahhhh Frankie, I already knew that you would. This is great. And it is less for you to worry about. In the future, if you want to find something just quiet your mind as best you can and listen to your intuition. But you are already doing that, aren't you, my love? I know how hard you work at being able to communicate with me.

F:
Do you hear me talking to you every day? And on my bike, and in my car?

L:
Yes, of course. How could I not? Our love of one another is keeping us linked up with our thoughts. Just don't forget to pay attention to the traffic! We don't want you to get hurt. Then I would have my hands full! Even from this side of things.

F:
Any messages you want me to give to anyone here for you?

L:
Tell Prince that I love him like a brother. That it is wonderful here. Not to pay any attention to any stories about heaven and hell that are negative. And to keep passing on the love to others . . . he can heal through his music, you know.

F:
I hope you are doing well there. I would like to hear more about it when we talk. Have you been able to hear me well when we talk directly?

L:
I am doing very well here . . . you have no idea. Everything is set up just right, just perfectly. All of our needs and desires are addressed. And yes, I hear you when you talk directly. LOVE makes sure of that.

F TO E:
Elizabeth, Wednesday, September 13th, is the one-year anniversary of Linda's passing. I hope it does not come up.

E:
I understand . . .

10/25/2023

F TO E:
Hi Elizabeth,
I'm looking forward to the call with you and Linda this Friday—they are so much fun!

I would like it if you can tell her a few things from me, and tell me what she says (or will we be on a recording?), because I can't hear what she says, and lately I have not been sure of my conversations with her. This darned anxiety reaction is still with me often, and it can disrupt my communication with her. Sorry to burden you with these subjects/questions, just do the best you can, all will be good.

E NOTE:
During my meditation, I had the experience of being told by spirit that Frank was having anxiety. "Spirit" in this case was a collective group of spirit people, not necessarily Linda:

The anxiety you are experiencing is an inevitable outcome of frustration over not being able to control the situation you have found yourself in. On the one hand, you are dealing with subtleties in the world of spirit which operate very differently from the way they do in Earth life, with its density in all things, operates. If you had many more years of experience operating with spirit, at least you would have had a deeper understanding of what to expect and how to work with the challenges faced when communicating with us when Linda made her transition.

In addition, some of the people you are working with on Earth, to accomplish tasks important to you, may not always respond in a timely manner. This further adds to your frustrations, leading to anxiety.

Thirdly, it is impossible to communicate with Linda in the way you had for decades as she no longer has a physical body. Know that your efforts to communicate with her are noted by us in spirit and we are doing everything we can to help facilitate that. Family and guides unite to help you. Understand that an acorn cannot grow into an oak tree quickly . . . it takes patience, the right amount of water, air, light, etc. What you have accomplished to date is extraordinary, something that most in your position cannot do. Linda and your loved ones in spirit are also being helped by us. There is much work going on in spirit as well as by you on Earth, to help facilitate communication between you and those in spirit.

F:
Linda, were you at the Beyond Baroque Gala last week? If so, did you see me?

L:
I'm always with you as your thoughts and your emotions are still connected to my thoughts and emotions. Our love is so strong, always has been and always will be. Death cannot stop that. Yes, I can see you even if you cannot see me. It is odd, is it not, that one can see the other but not always the other way around? This is because from my position my body is finer and of a higher vibration. It is also frustrating to me, but I am getting used it. Also, I am learning to navigate your world in a way that sends some sort of message to you.

F:
Quentin Ring, the Director, mentioned you and your scholarship you created for women poets from the stage.

L:
Yes, it is exciting! I am so grateful that because of you my beloved, others may be helped to pursue poetry. I can't express how much this means to me. Thank you thank you for helping to set this up.

F:
Do you get Earth news where you are?

L:
Yes, we do. We get updates from other spirit people who are constantly monitoring the Earth as well as from those who also visit loved ones. I also pick up on Earth news through your thoughts and experiences even if you are not aware. We often get Earth news before you do! Not only that, even before it happens on Earth! Especially major events and/or events pertaining to loved ones on Earth. How else would we be able to occasionally intervene to help people

during times of crisis? We know beforehand and are there in spirit to help those in need to get through life's vicissitudes.

F:
I believe you told me you have a pet, no?

E:
(At this point, I perceive a picture of Linda holding a small dog. Not the smallest kind of dog but small enough to hold like a cat is held. It is of a light color. Linda and the dog are really enjoying each other and appear to be very, very happy.)

F:
Did you go to dinner with me (Frank) and our Herbalife friends, Greco, Patty, et al?

L:
I popped in to see what you were eating.

E:
(Then she relays to me something about laughing, jokes or people just having a good time. She liked the sense of humor. It made her feel good to see you around others with good energies, warmness. She stayed a while and *"knew that you would be all right."*)

F:
Are you going with me to Sheila Pinkel's home for Thanksgiving again this year?

F TO E:
FYI: The photo of Linda in front of the fireplace I sent you in late September was taken in Sheila Pinkel's home.

L:
Of course I am, Frank!

E:
(I "see" a big fat turkey on a platter being held by a woman. Lots of good company and *"hehe good spirits!"*)

L:
I am looking forward to it.

F:
I think you know about the three projects I am doing in your name, no? The scholarship is pretty well set up. Now it's onward with the book, and your archives.

L:
I do wish you would slow down. As much as I appreciate all your efforts on my behalf, I hate to see you overworked. Yes, I am aware of the projects . . . maybe some young poet or artist will find those archives useful.

F TO E:
That's it, Liz. You can ask these in any order you see fit. There is a lot I'd like to know about how she is doing there, and a lot I would like to tell her about what's going on here. I guess I don't know enough about her life there yet to ask good questions.
    Thanks for your help.
    Frank

E COMMENTS:
In this communication, more spirit people are making themselves known to Frank through their communications to him.

F COMMENTS:
Yes, and the first part of this Reading session can give you a good way of understanding how things work in the Afterlife, how our DLOs learn and adapt to their new world, which ultimately we will do.

11/15/2023

F:
Have we been communicating lately? Have I been getting through to you?

L:
Yes, even when you are unaware of it, we still are communicating. Often through your unconscious or subconscious states of awareness. This is because sometimes your waking consciousness unintentionally interferes. For example, you have a strong personality with strong thoughts. You have been like this for most of your adult life. However, our communications to you are very subtle and the "love cable" (so to speak) is unable to respond in a way your full consciousness recognizes.

They tell me that this is a tricky business. Because, dear one, sometimes enthusiasm presents an emotion that interferes. The mind needs to be clear and relaxed. There is a such a thing as trying too hard. This is a very different mindset than that used when working with the rational mind. If you could just relax and let it organically happen with less effort on your end, you might be surprised.

Trying to control the outcome, for example, being able to specifically contact me as if we are using a telephone, interferes with spirits' efforts to commune with you. If you could try to be more open to whatever spirit offers, you may find it easier to connect with me. It is all up to spirit and sometimes what spirit decides is in the best interests of the recipient is not what the recipient expects or understands. That is all right, it has always been that way.

F TO E:
There is a possibility that my mom and/or Dad might make an appearance, as they have been familiar and good with Linda by now. I would like them to know how much I love them, and how lucky I am to have them as my parents. Every day I think of the lessons they taught me. If Dad is nearby, I have had the feeling that he wants to talk to me; I know Mom does. We will see how it goes. They are both great people.

FRANK'S FATHER:
Yes, I want to talk to you about communication with us. The importance of letting go and how that works in your favor in the long run . . . we do help some people when they come over here to adjust. And, I have been here a long time by your Earth measurements and have learned a thing or two about this subject . . . your activities have encouraged me to learn more. Your mother is also learning but I will leave that up to her to explain.

F TO E:
As to Linda, ditto on the love and lucky me part, as I feel very lucky to have her in my life and want her to know that. She is the most wonderful person I have ever met, and I loved our lives together.
   I would like to know from Linda: What projects are you involved in now?

L:
Still playing music, singing, helping mom, helping you (yes Frank, you are one of my projects now), composing poetry. I sometimes like to observe new people settling in, what they go through, etc. Fascinating. Sometimes they vacillate between this world and yours until they are finally adjusted enough to stay here permanently.

F:
How is your recent "healing" going? How are your eyes?

L:
My eyes are healthy. It didn't take long to get a new set. Bam! I'm over here and I experienced the most amazing healings of my new body. A few months, if that, and I felt perfectly new.

F:
How are you feeling?

L:
Wiser than I was on Earth. I am constantly learning new things and developing new ways of understanding life on Earth and life here in spirit. You have

played a large role in this through your never ending and consistent interest/efforts in wanting to communicate with me. It encourages me to understand how this kind of communication works . . . which leads to greater understanding of many things. Human auras, for example. Now that I can "see" them, they are like an energy field about the Earth human body, I can really experience how it is that souls in physical bodies really are "spiritual beings" having a "physical experience."

F:
Anything else you want to tell me?
   Do you sing around your house there, like you did when we were together?

E:
It's on the recording.

F:
Do you sit around your house?

L:
Only if I should tire which doesn't happen that much these days. There are too many exciting and beautiful things to do here. Besides, a certain man by the name of Frank from Earth, keeps ringing my etheric phone. I pick up but he can't hear me . . . but I hear him! I am not serious about the etheric phone but we do have humorous names for connecting with loved ones on Earth. Like the "love cable."

E COMMENTS:
Linda communicates that not only does life continue after the great transition but so does learning and developing.

F COMMENTS:
Ditto the above, and the way life continues is full of vibrancy, and as several of the books I have read explain, love and helpfulness among the various inhabitants.

12/13/2023

F:
Did you get my message about Alex and me copying a bunch of your old poetry and performance videos to give to the Getty Museum and Beyond Baroque?

L:
Yes, I did!! How exciting! A lot of work on your and Alex's part! It's actually a little funny to realize that those videos of me will live on in perpetuity as I never even thought of such a thing while on Earth. Thank you, Frank from the bottom of my heart, thank you, my love.

F:
Do you celebrate Christmas there?

L:
I am glad you asked, Frankie. Christmas can be an interesting time here, if I may be permitted to use the phrase "time". This is partly dependent upon where one ends up as "my father's mansion has many rooms". In other words, there are people here from many faiths, all faiths actually. We tend to "collect" ourselves with groups/places where we feel most comfortable. For me, that is a place with a Christian Judaic feel to it; however, we really don't adhere to any one religion and as we spiritually grow here, we can move to a different neighborhood where the backgrounds of the spirit people differ more.

In any case, this time of year we can feel the celebrations of many different peoples coming from the Earth. There is Christmas, the New Year, Hanukkah, etc. The Earth vibrations during this time of the year . . . the Earth's winter solstice . . . can be felt by us here in the world of spirit. Because Earth's vibrations can be higher than other times of the year, it is easier for us to connect and communicate with you all. So, it is not so much that we celebrate Christmas as is done on Earth as it is a recognized time of Earth, by us in spirit, in which the conditions on Earth are more favorable towards higher vibrations.

Your joy is our joy. Your generosity towards others is felt as a sweet vibratory sensation, like sweet musical tones, here in heaven. Many of us understand not to limit ourselves to any one religion for the true picture is much greater, much more immense. This time of year has been celebrated by all peoples in the Northern Hemisphere of Earth, ever since the dinosaurs! This is when the sun returns. And when a celebration is had that recognizes the light within people. This light being the product of spiritual development throughout the rest of the year.

F:
Are you writing a book of short stories about people?

L:
I must confess not really, as I am inundated with reading the writings of others. Still settling in as there is so much to do here! I am still focusing on music and singing. People love to hear me sing and make music; especially those who are newcomers. I find music and song to be so magical here because of the effect it can have on others through vibration. It is more than just hearing sound . . . the sounds sound different than on Earth, they are richer and of an infinite range of notes. And an infinite range of notes between the notes. And they have a fragrance attached to them! Yes, you heard that right . . . these sounds can have a fragrance just as flowers do, almost like their own aura in the form of a scent. And we can feel the vibrations of the sounds. And often see the color associated with each sound. Passing on music and song to others is far more dynamic than merely writing something . . . though there is a place and purpose for that as well. Think of the heavenly stars, Frank, the Milky Way and beyond. There is a sense of infinity and immensity beyond human comprehension, even beyond my spirit comprehension. The beauty is beyond description.

F:
Have you seen Alberta (Linda's Mom) or my mom and dad lately?

L:
I do see them occasionally as they are in the neighborhood, so to speak. I think of them or they of me, and pop! We are together. But I am getting better at standing on my own as time progresses, which is a good thing. All of us have so many activities to pursue while over here . . .

E:
It's on the recording.

E NOTE:
Added while we were talking on the phone that Linda communicated it has to do with time and distance being different on the other side. On Earth it is very dense (i.e., our physical bodies), the atmosphere, the planet.

F:
A lot of our friends want me to say hello and send you love from them!

L:
I feel their good wishes, often. Sometimes I even visit them whether or not they can sense me.

F:
Do you know—that Jim Turrell called me yesterday Tuesday, asked about you, sends a kiss and his love to you.

L:
Yes, yes, yes! I felt his love as I was discussed by you two. He was/is always such a creative man, with a creative and open mind. He expresses his love with his art projects on large scales. I think maybe his sense of space is very great, due to his flying experiences. This is why he ties his creativity into the Earth, expressing his energy on a large scale. That is his heart we are looking at, when he creates art and buildings . . . he listens to the land.

F TO E:
Liz, Turrell is one of our best friends, and my flying partner; we go back to 1968. He's the famous American artist with the volcano project in Arizona.

E COMMENTS:
If one is not familiar with Turrell's artistry, it is worth looking it up on the Internet. His work is truly a treat to see.

12/28/2023

F:
FYI: Linda, who is usually upbeat, is a bit sad that we can't be together during these Holidays—and I am feeling sad about it, too. I think/hope that my communicating with her can help her, as it helps me to talk to her.

L:
I always look forward to our communications and I hope that today's will uplift you as much as it uplifts me. Since it always uplifts me, it should be a good day, my love. Christmas time is tough, especially for those who have lost someone near and dear, that they always spent the holidays with. That goes for us, my dear. But like all things, it passes and as the new year approaches and begins its journey, things will change, broaden, and brighten upon the landscape of living. This will help you, us together, in communing, living our respective lives albeit one of us without a physical body. What pains me the most is when I see you suffer on my account.

There are others, here on this side, that become sad during the holidays that are celebrated on Earth. It is well understood by those who have been in spirit longer than us newcomers. People here are so accommodating and understanding towards those of us still struggling to let go of these things of Earth. So, no worries . . . I am in very good hands with spirit people working on our behalf . . . yours and mine . . . to get us through the Northern Earth's holidays, then onward and forward to the light. For the light is not just for us on this side of things, but also for the people of the Earth. Frank, I see how you have grown spiritually since I parted (though I really haven't left you, as you know). And I know how you are working to share your light with others! I am so excited about this. Your writing about after death communications, specifically, and sharing it in workshops will touch others in ways you cannot anticipate. Every little bit helps in getting the message out to Earth, that life does not end when the physical body ends. Not in the least! What does happen is that life continues, consciousness continues . . .

F:
What color flowers do you want now, if not red?

L:
Red is always my favorite. Blue . . . if you can find it but that is a very rare flower color. If you can't find a blue flower, then draw one or better yet send me one in thought. I will receive it with glory!

You know, Frank, you just need to think of a flower, of gifting me one, and in thought and heart I will receive it. I always appreciate when you pick up physical flowers for me, but that is not a requirement. What I am trying to convey is that your mind and heart can produce flowers for me.

If only you could see the flowers here where I am. The colors are indescribable as there are vibrant colors here that Earth does not have. The higher vibrations that we live under make this possible. And many flowers emanate a light of their own, like an aura. Imagine, not only do these kinds of flowers emit a fragrance beyond description, but they can also emit light!

F:
I miss you and think about you very much every day, and love you as I always have, and I always will love you. You are my source of joy!

L:
Oh Frankie, I can't wait 'til we meet again both of us, in this world. But not a second before your time. This is very important. As you still have much to learn from the world of Earth and in helping others. You are already reaching out to others, telling them the truth about life after death. But yes, you are always on my mind as I love you too, dearly . . . and always will. I so feel your love for me as I am here in spirit. Waiting, my love, waiting. Though not a moment, not a second too soon. (**E:** I am hearing the song "You Were Always on My Mind" by Willie Nelson.)

F:
Are you able to see what I have written about you in the book of our poetry and stories that I am working on publishing?

L:
Yes, of course. I pick up on it through our minds and hearts. You make me blush! Imagine a spirit person blushing! That is like a blushing ghost. (**E:** I hear Linda laugh.) *You seem to know no bounds in praising me. Ahhh, geez Frank, I don't know if I deserve all that, but I want you to know how much I appreciate it. Ours is a real love story . . .* (**E:** then Linda communicates something about a story about Africa . . . her visits there with her friend with the Kora instrument, Prince Diabate, and Frank. And working with the local people too.)

F:
Suzanne Lummis has written and posted a beautiful tribute to you in her Facebook page, and, so far, it has generated over 160 beautiful tributes to you from other people, including other artists and people who don't know you.

L:
Dear Suzanne . . . she was always such a good friend. I cannot believe the reactions of so many on my behalf. If only I could reach out to each and every one with a spirit hug so they would personally experience me, from the world of spirit, just how much their efforts are appreciated by me. It is so touching. Suzanne touches me in my heart. Such a dear woman.

F:
Suzanne is also writing another tribute to you, soon to be published in *Poetry Flash*.

L:
It seems I am becoming a bit of a celebrity there! Here is a little secret . . . sometimes I help both you and Suzanne in what you/she write. Not always . . . but yes to some degree. I wish you could see how things work here. It is so different. People's hearts, their emotions, as well as their thoughts, can be felt and perceived by everyone else. There are no secrets. We are what our thoughts and emotions are.

F:

You were able to contact Leslie directly. Do you still find it difficult to contact me directly? If so, what can I do to make it easier for you to contact me? I feel like you are always with me.

L:

Just keep being Frank, doing what you are already doing in terms of effort to connect with me. The flower within you will continue to grow and communication will become easier. I am always with you! That is why you feel I am always with you.

01/24/2024

F:
Linda, do you remember the year of the last performance of Nearly Fatal Women?

E:
We talked about this during the phone call, that I was not able to get a year.

F:
Your Linda Week at Beyond Baroque will begin on Saturday, April 13th. I am getting made a bunch of 3-inch "Linda's face" buttons to hand out to the crowd.

L:
Oh Frank, this is too funny. People might think we are in love! What would the neighbors think?

E:
(I hear Linda laughing.)

F:
Do you sometimes visit your studio in "D" to see your archives we have arranged?

L:
I am often there when you are there.

E:
(I see two people in a room handling objects that look like papers or CDs . . . not sure what the objects are. I then see someone handling an old-fashioned tape used to record sound. The tape is not completely wound up. Some of it is loose.)

L:
I usually don't visit the studio without you or the presence of the two people. It is through your thoughts and love that I am able to go to certain physical places on Earth, like the studio in "D". There have been times when I have visited on my

own because your thoughts and emotions have been focused there. Even after you have visited physically, or non-physically through your thoughts, a certain "residue" remains with you which I can use to visit if I want to.

When you "think", combined with emotion which in this case is love, it creates a kind of energetic link that I can follow along to connect with the "object in question" on Earth. You are literally creating a nonphysical connection or cable if you like. You can't see it or feel it, but me, being without a physical body like yours, can work easily with this kind of connection.

We use our minds, our intentions, our focus when we want to connect. I can be with you while still being here "on the other side". It is our consciousness that is doing the traveling.

I know you have been busy working in the studio in "D", on my behalf. I am with you, doing my best to help with thoughts, ideas, and inspiration while you work.

E:
(I see Linda placing her hand on Frank's back in a comforting manner.)

F:
Have you seen the new blue flowers I got for you?

E:
(I see Linda standing and holding a vase of flowers, they are smaller in size and remind me of forget-me-nots. She smiles as she holds the flowers, and she looks proud of what you got her. She says something about Valentine's Day. I am being impressed that Linda is trying make a connection with the flowers and the holiday season. I hear music playing in my mind "She Wore Blue Velvet". Then I hear *"Blue flowers are hard to find!"* and *"Thank you. I love them."*)

F:
Is it you making my lights blink on and off?

L:
My team and I have been experimenting with different ways to communicate with you. So yes, there is a group of us working on your behalf to make

connections. They say I am easy to work with in this regard because of my past interests in such communications and your own deep desire and willingness and interest. So, the atmosphere in your home and around you, sets up good conditions for such fun/phenomena.

E:
(I see a single feather falling.)

L:
I already had a group in spirit that were with me while I was on Earth. They helped to bring us together, you and me Frank, when we first met! This same group are now helping us, really, to connect. As we connect, thoughts about connecting with spirit go out and about the planet and add to the growing momentum that is pushing Earth people to better understand that life continues after death.

Your parents often times join us in our efforts. They are very interested in how all this works. Your father in particular is fascinated . . . I think your mom isn't as interested in the methods as her heart already knows this is possible.

F:
Can you visit me in my dreams?

L:
I can and do, you just aren't remembering the dreams! You may, on occasion, see me in a dream or while you are in a dream like state. I come across as a flash. That is me sending you a signal that I am with you in thought, in mind and heart!

F:
Have you come across any old friends there?

E:
(I see a dark-toned women in what appears to be traditional African clothing. She appears like a flash I see her so briefly. There is cotton cloth wrapped around her body like a dress but not exactly a dress, and also around her head. [Wanda Coleman?]

There is also a woman who briefly flashes in, a Euro-American. She was older, maybe when she passed? [Jackie Apple?]

While Frank and I talk on the phone, I describe more of the Euro-American lady and we decide it is probably "Jackie".)

F:
I'm looking for your LA Harbour poems—any idea where they are?

E:
(Frank tells me that he found them.)

F:
Linda, are you around me much? I can't tell . . .

L:
I am around more than you realize. You may not be able to tell, but I am there. If you could but stop thinking in terms of four dimensions and its limitations, that might help your mind to more easily accept that I am around you often. I am not limited by the physical body. I am not limited by time and space like you are. In this way, I readily experience communications with you.

01/29/2024

F:
I think you told me you went to Germany recently—I'm jealous! I always wanted to take you there! Next time, we will go together. I will take you to Rothenburg, where the earliest use of the family name Lutz is recorded.

E:
(As I read this, I am shown by spirit a tombstone in a graveyard, presumably having a connection to your family in some way.)

L:
It is not easy at first to be able to visit places on Earth. There is a sense of double duty when one first arrives in spirit land ... wanting to visit Europe and also wanting to settle in my new land (of the spirit world). But, once I realized it is all mind and all I need do is to think it, then I can transport my consciousness to different places on the Earth. In this case it was Germany. Your parents helped me along in this endeavor. And it was they who showed me the cemetery with the tombstone. Someday, when the time and conditions are right, we can visit together.

E:
(As I type this, I am also shown a small home which reminds me of a large cottage, slopping roof, porch, somewhere high up like a mountainous region with a lake. Feels cold but good cold, like fresh air.)

F:
How do you travel long distance—by teleportation, or astral projection, or by your imagination, or flying yourself, or what?

L:
It is through thought and consciousness akin to what is sometimes called astral travels, out of body travels, etc. You can do this too, but it would be more difficult for you as you still have your physical body. Without an Earthly physical body, the constraints of time and distance are diminished, practically

non-existent, at least how it is experienced on Earth. Hence, we can "travel" where we wish. It sort of feels like a "whoosh" at first. A bit unsettling but one gets used to it very quickly. You think it, define it when you think it and you can be there. Not everyone likes to visit the Earth, though. I thought you might find this interesting. Many here are quite settled into their new lives and are quite busy living that. Visiting Earth comes with a sense of density which for many here can be a challenge. There is the risk of reliving old pains and sorrows and one must be developed enough so that risk is very small to nothing.

There are many on Earth who are good at projecting their conscious awareness at great distances. Some have written books about their experiences.

By the way, when we visit loved ones on Earth, there often is a blending into the loved one's aura which can have a certain amount of protection about it. I don't know if protection is the most accurate word, but it is what I have to work with at the moment.

F:
What kind of social activities does the population have there where you are?

L:
The same you have one Earth! Friends, family, come to visit and I go to their places. Getting involved in various activities provides ample opportunity to meet new people. Sometimes just walking around and looking at the city, the new land I am in, allows me to meet new people too, to socialize with.

E:
(Spirit is showing me a beautiful dirt pathway about ten feet wide with trees with lots of green leaves and many birds flying about.)

F:
Your clothes—do you just imagine what you want to wear and it happens?

L:
I wear what I feel most comfortable in! Today it is pants. Tomorrow it may be a robe. People who have been here a long time prefer more generic spirit clothing (so to speak) which may appear as robe like. But many of us newbies

(relatively speaking) still cling to clothing we felt most comfortable in while on Earth. Sometimes I will even wear a dress but usually casual pants. When I visit you, I always will appear in something that you can recognize as something I would wear.

E:
(Linda is jokingly showing herself to me. She is wearing a bathing suit that looks like a yellow bikini!)

L:
If I want, I can imagine myself in a particular set of clothes, but I prefer to just wear whatever covers me without thinking much about it. We don't usually like to be bothered worrying about, troubling ourselves, with what to wear. That's why at some point people who have been here a while sometimes prefer the more generic spirit clothes.

F:
Have you been having trouble connecting with me? I have had trouble connecting with you.

L:
It is always easier for me to connect with you. I am not being constrained by a physical body which is subject to the laws of physics on Earth which contain inherently time and space. Your trouble connecting with me is due more to your being new at such communications, your being in a physical body. Also, your grief. You are doing tremendous work in increasing your psychic abilities to connect with the world of spirit so do not underestimate yourself. Often times, when you are trying to connect with me, I am there and saying, "Frank, here I am. I am with you in thought and love with you right now." In other words, you are successful in connecting with me, but your own consciousness is not aware of it! I realize how frustrating this is for you but please have faith in me, that I am there. Your physical senses are there for a purpose. But I am there more often than you will ever be able to sense at this point in time. Your body is simply not ready at this point to sense as much as you would like it to. That's because there are still things on Earth that you need to experience . . .

F:
Do you sleep at night (evening), or just take short naps?

L:
In the beginning, I did do what you call sleep a lot because I was still transitioning into the new world. As I am here longer, I no longer need to do that so much. Night sleeping . . . we really don't have a nighttime as you know it. It is sunny most or all of the time. Our bodies (yes, we have bodies that are physical but not in the way you experience physical bodies on the Earth), don't require sleep. It is our minds and hearts though that need rest. It depends on the activities we are involved in. It is more like we regularly slow down and rest. When we do sleep, sometimes we can go and visit other spirit worlds like the higher ones. That is because the bodies we have here where I am are denser than those in higher places where mind and emotion are even more subtle than here.

F:
You told me some time ago that you had met Edgar Degas, the great French Impressionist painter, at a local art show. Have you seen him or any other notables since then?

E:
(She is showing me a group of people within which are other "great artists", maybe one or two. I don't recognize them as I am not familiar with the art world all that much. I sense "movement" about the place in terms of meeting different types of spirit people.)

L:
It is a matter of need, curiosity, desire. When it is helpful for me to meet a person whose skill I am interested in, and that person is available to meet, then somehow it comes together and we meet. Interestingly, artistic ability requires a certain amount of sensitivity to the world of spirit. They are inspired to create beautiful work. Their minds and hearts blend with spirit to work on their creations. So over here, depending on circumstances, a spirit artist may have a stencil or paintbrush and paint to create something using their hands. But in other cases, it can be more of a "thinking" the creation of an art. Everyone is

unique and everyone works a little differently. In the case of Degas, he demonstrated to us the use of light and thought to create paintings. The colors that resulted are indescribable. They emit a light! And a sound that some of us can hear if we wish to. It is a blending of more than one perceptive spirit sense that results in this kind of experience.

F:
Are you able to communicate with Spirit Guides to ask them to help you contact me? Just know—I have always loved you and always will—you are my favorite person in all worlds. I will be so happy to be with you again!

L:
What you call Spirit Guides, well not exactly. There are spirit people here who are better skilled at communicating with Earth than the typical person. So, they help us, help me to do so. It is usually a group endeavor. But I can do it on my own too. It is just that with more than one spirit involved, there is more energy in the communication/connection, so you are more likely to perceive me.

F:
Linda told me that recently she had been to Paris, and walked some of the streets she and I had walked together, and then Italy, where we had been. She also told me she had visited Chicago (I think Chicago). When she travels, do you think it is via something like astral projection, or by flying herself (they can move at the speed of light!), or what?

E:
This was addressed earlier. See above.

02/05/2024

F:
Linda, thank you for the wonderful life and love we have had together for so many years, and I look forward to many more years with you where you are now!

L:
My dear Frank, love is never something that stops or dies simply because the physical body has been shed. Love is eternal. Our love is like a reflection of the great universal love . . . I have no words to describe this. We will indeed be together when the time comes. I will be there to help you transition, and there will be others there, like your parents and your own Spirit Guides. It will be a great celebration!

When I first left the Earth, it was so difficult for me to be without you. But after a while, after I settled into my new home and began to understand the bigger picture of existence and consciousness, this is when I began to experience time differently. It is so different than how it is experienced on Earth. What may seem to you to be an infinite period of time is, to us, a very short period. This is hard to explain. I just know that when the time is right, the time is right. And I accept this and am at peace with it.

We here understand that this is difficult for our counterparts on Earth to comprehend. I am referring to how different is our experience of time than that of people on Earth. In a sense, we have much more patience and acceptance that everything has a cycle, and that cycle cannot be shortened. It just is.

We will be together my love, I promise. When the cycle runs its course. In the meantime, continue spreading the concept of life after death, that our consciousness continues after the physical body ceases, and that it is indeed possible to continue our relations between the two worlds . . . but that it is just different.

F:
Have you seen my Ohio State football pictures I put out for you on the dining room table? I was 18 years old at the time the photos were taken.

E:
(I am being impressed with the idea that Linda did indeed see these pictures, or at least one or two of them, while she was on Earth, and she is seeing them again but this time from the Afterlife.)

L:
Frank, you are a riot! Yes, I can see them through my mind. Especially when you have it in your mind that you want me to see them. Thoughts are actual things. And when there is something that you very much want me to know about, our strong love enables those thoughts to travel along our "love cable" (so to speak) and reach me. Then the image of your football pictures can arrive in my mind. Thoughts are real. Emotions are real. Thoughts and love make it possible for us to communicate between the two worlds. How wonderful this is.

I would like to add that every time you do something like this, it helps me to connect with you. This is because of "intent". Intent creating thought along with love or emotion, that enables the intended thought to reach me. This includes your football pictures, flowers you bought for me, lapel buttons, activities on my behalf, activities that are important to you, etc. Yes, even activities that are not necessarily intended for me but are important to you can also help us to connect. This is because we have a very deep, emotional bond with one another, a bond that does not end when the physical body no longer works. It is a psychic bond, as in psyche or soul . . . the ancient meaning.

F:
You were recently asking me not to work so hard. I hope you heard the reasons for my doing so: that I am your loyal and loving husband, champion, and pal, your "backup", and that you and your wonderful art need to be remembered by the public. Also, that in the future, people who are now living on Earth will be joining us where you are, and it will be good that some of them will know your name and your art when they meet you.

L:
When Frank makes up his mind, Frank makes up his mind. You always did have a stubborn streak in you, which I admired. One of the things I loved about you even if at times it could be exasperating!

You are in a sense, demonstrating to others who are still on Earth how it is possible to remain connected with loved ones who have passed.

I still think you should slow down. If it is meant for people living on Earth to someday connect with me in the other worlds, it will happen regardless. Nonetheless, your work on my behalf is very much appreciated. You always treated me so well . . .

F:
I met with Quentin Ring and Suzanne Thompson last Saturday to plan your birthday celebration at Beyond Baroque in April. I told them you will be there. They both adore you, and we talked a lot about you and your art(s).

E:
(I see Linda doing what looks like a happy dance. She says, *"We're gonna have a party, a party! Yes!"* She is impressing me with the idea of memories of good old times, past parties, and celebrations.)

L:
I will be there in mind and heart . . . if you sense me, it will not be your, nor Quentin's, nor Suzanne's imagination. When two or more are gathered in his name, so shall I be there . . . this biblical quote also applies to any group of people gathering on Earth in the name of someone who has transitioned. Life does continue!

F:
I am having made some beautiful lapel buttons with your beautiful face on them and your name under your face to hand out to the crowd who comes.

L:
Flattery will get you everywhere! I hope you picked out a good picture of me when my hair looked great and not messed up. I would not want my public to see me when I was not at my best.

E:
(I see Linda from the shoulders up with her hair all messed up and kind of looking like Albert Einstein, *"If they see me like this, then I would have to do mathematical equations which I can't do!"*)

F:
I try to talk to you every day, but some days I don't know if I am getting through to you. Do you usually hear me daily?

L:
Yes, your love carries your thoughts created by your words to me every time. Look for small signs . . . they will be there. It is always easier for us to be aware of your thoughts than it is for you to be able to perceive us. This has to do with dimensionality (which I have been looking into as we can attend lectures and talks by many learned people). It is like someone living in a two-dimensional world cannot perceive the world in three dimensions, whereas someone living in a three-dimensional world can indeed perceive someone in a two-dimensional world. You are like someone living in a four-dimensional world (width, length, height, and time) while I am in a fifth dimensional world. I see you! Can you see me?

E:
(I hear her laughing and am impressed with Linda as if she is playing peekaboo with a child.)

L:
As you unfold your non-physical senses, you temporarily move into a more multidimensional state of awareness and hence, can become more aware of my thoughts, feelings, messages, etc. All is thought . . . well sort of, as love plays a large component.

F:
I got you new flowers in the living room.

L:
And of course I am aware of this. These flowers, they have an aura about them that is like the scent of flowers but is not experienced as a scent. It is more like an energetic field. Embedded in this field I can sense your love. Think of a flower's scent emanating outward but instead of a scent, it is energy comprised of love. It extends outward, invisible to the physical senses and yet is surely there.

F:
I have to start working on taxes. OMG!!

L:
Don't talk to me about taxes. That is one of the things of Earth that I do not miss. Make sure you take a break and have plenty of beer to get you through this horrible mess of an experience. There are no taxes here! (**E:** I hear Linda laughing again.) *I love you, Frank. Don't let the bastards get you down when doing those taxes.*

F TO E:
To be honest with you, I would really like to ask Linda what she is up to these days, what projects have her occupied? I know she wants to hear what is going on in my/her world here at home, but I don't want to ignore her activities in the Afterlife.

L:
Our activities in this new world of mine, as it is for all of us here, always involve the concept of service to others. This is very important for we continue to progress here, spiritually, emotionally, and mentally. And the surest way to progress in the realm of spirit is in serving others. We are, in short, serving spirit. Although people on Earth often refer to us as "spirits", we have the concept of something greater than ourselves but is yet still part of reality. This "something greater" is more apparent to us after we have transitioned. So, we serve Spirit with a capital "S" by serving others.

We start with those talents and abilities which we used on Earth and build on them in order to serve Spirit by serving others. This brings a great measure of happiness and joy that is hard to describe with mere words. In my case, I have a vast experience with the art world (i.e., poetry, dance, performance, song and music). I use it to help soothe the "souls" (so to speak) of people here in need. Sometimes I will write poetry that is even customized, if you will, for a particular individual in a particular need. Kind of like a doctor's prescription. Using words to heal.

They first taught me to use my poetry to help me heal myself when I first arrived. Then, as part of my healing I also began writing for specific people as well as for groups. Music, I have also learned to use in a similar way to help heal others. But even if others are not in need of healing, still, music, being a universal language, is used to simply bring about joy and happiness in others, as well as a greater awareness of the spirit, as in the Great Spirit, that abounds about us and without which we would not exist. Much of this work is to bring a greater awareness to others and myself, an awareness that extends beyond the confines of mind and emotion. As for the physical body, we don't have one as we did on Earth. But we do have a body that is made of finer material and is just as real, perhaps more so, than the Earth body. That too, we strive to focus less on while striving to focus more on the greater things that created the very universe and of which no words can suffice to describe.

F NOTE:
I asked if I could kiss her hand there, as I always did here on Earth. She said, *"Don't worry! I am solid enough that you can feel my hand!"* She loved it whenever I kissed her hand!

02/21/2024

F:
Linda, I feel lost without you, it's no fun here for me. Am I getting through to you when we talk one-on-one directly?

L:
Yes, you are. I know it must be frustrating for you as it is for me. You cannot hear me like I can hear you. You send me your thoughts through your words as you talk to me and I assure you, I can hear them. But when I try to respond to let you know this, the thought doesn't always get through to you. Your thoughts come from a denser zone than where I am. So, I can perceive them. The lighter zone can perceive the denser zone. But the denser zone cannot as easily perceive the lighter zone (at least not without proper development and even then, there are problems). Where I am now, our bodies are less dense, the atmosphere is less dense, our thoughts and emotions consequently are less dense. We are made from a finer material than what Earth is made from.

The same analogy would hold for dimensions. I come from a place with more than the traditional four dimensions which make up time and location. You come from a place of four dimensions (time, length, width, and height).

Keep in mind that when we speak of dimensions, it is more like a continuum than a discrete difference. Consciousness plays a large role in this.

Love plays a large role in this, as it makes such communications possible. Love is of a higher frequency; that is the nature of love. Our love for one another, combined with our thoughts, make communication possible.

So, to answer your question, yes, I hear you talking to me. Sometimes it can be frustrating when I hear you talking to me because you can't perceive that I am. I want you to hear me, sense me, etc. Nonetheless, the development you've accomplished in a short period of time in being receptive to spirit, is greatly appreciated by me. I love you, Frank, so much! You were and still are the best husband a girl could ever dream of.

F:
Kat and Peter send you love, so does everybody else as I talk about you often.

E:
(As I read about Kat and Peter sending their love to Linda, I feel Kat and Peter's love in my physical heart.)

L:
Actually, I felt their love when you typed up this message before sending it to the medium. In fact, I felt it in your unconscious mind even before you wrote it. I am not constricted by the concept of time as is Earth. We are aware of things happening even before they happen! It does get weird at times. I love being able to communicate with you this way . . .

F:
Your Beyond Baroque Linda Fellowship is on their web page and looks great!

L:
Yes, and it is so exciting! I will be there with you! I will be there at the festival. By now you shouldn't expect less of me.

E:
(She blows a kiss through the ethers for Frank.)

F:
Do you hear me talk to you as I walk up Speedway Alley, past 11 Wavecrest to get my car?

L:
I'm always there with you. I am like a ripple in the ethers, in the air, in the atmosphere of Earth Land. (**E:** I hear Linda laughing.) *That is funny as "Earth Land" is a play on words for the book "Flat Land" because that is what Earth is like to us. My five-dimensional world of spirit encompasses your four-dimensional world of Earth. So, you cannot perceive me in the way you usually perceive the things of Earth. Like the continuum described above, the more you develop your psychic abilities, the more likely you are to sense me during such occasions.*

    A point of mention . . . sometimes it is indeed possible for spirit to get a message across to someone on Earth even if the recipient is not developed psychically. When this happens, more than one of us usually act as a team in tandem. It makes for a stronger battery or generator than can penetrate the Earth's atmosphere more efficiently.

It all comes down to mind, it is all mind. And love.

F:
Have you seen Jackie Apple? Or Wanda Coleman?

E:
(I see an African American woman, who is wearing a button with Linda's picture on it. This woman is proud of the button.)

F:
Do you hear me in my classes with Elizabeth, our lady medium?

L:
Oh Frank! I work with her closely to get messages to you. I work with her and her spirit team before your sessions while she works on your questions. I work with her during your one-on-one sessions on the phone. And of course, I work with her during her classes. I can pick up the other students' energies! It can be very interesting. I am, at once, with you in California but with them in Connecticut, too. It is as if we all form a circle in the ethers with our subtle bodies. I am there, you are there, the students and the lady medium are there. So is her spirit team, the other students' team, people and family for me, the students, you, the medium . . . it is fascinating to experience people on Earth doing this work with us here in heaven. It is always an experiment. Each workshop is different with different energies. Adjustments are made to the students' minds and subtle bodies to better prepare them for mediumship.

F:
My desire is to see you more often with clairvoyance, and to see you in my dreams.

L:
You will, Frank, you will. But it takes time and practice. Be grateful for what you do perceive even if it is not clairvoyantly. Spirit knows what is best for you. The

flower can't be forced to bloom. Take it one day at a time. I so want you to be able to see me too! Close your eyes and imagine me . . . and there I will be waiting for you. I am but a step away.

F:
The other day I saw you outside leaning against a fence—do you remember our talk?

L:
You said you love me, you miss me. You talked about upcoming activities related to Beyond Baroque and your parents. You said you are glad my mother is there with me and asked why can't we be together.

F:
Do you feel like writing a poem, dictating it to me, and having me present it here for you at Beyond Baroque, and explaining its origin to the audience?

E NOTE:
Frank explained to me what he meant by the question. I agreed with Frank that if he were to write poetry by Linda (by channeling her), it would be a very delicate situation in sharing this with others, such as the Beyond Baroque crowd. Also, that they might misinterpret Frank's intentions. Frank said he would probably speak with one of his colleagues for feedback on how to possibly handle this.

03/08/2024

F:
Is it OK to talk to you out loud from the confines of my living room—or would you rather I do it in my head?

L:
Absolutely it is OK! In fact, it helps to make the communication that much stronger. Your voice has its own particular frequency which gets imparted into space around you; both the physical space as well as the space that is non-material. In other words, by speaking your words out loud, you are strengthening your psychic battery-generator (so to speak) in a way that sends out stronger signals through the ethers to reach me. Never be afraid to speak to me out loud (except in front of other people . . . but you know this of course, I need not say this).

Why do you think song was invented? Music is the language of the Gods . . . song is word put to even a higher vibration in music form. When you speak out loud to me, your voice helps raise up your thought-forms to the other worlds. It is like giving your thought-forms wings! Song is beautiful, your words are beautiful, "for they are as a song in poetry is to me". Your words, your thoughts are carried to me through your love. My heart (**E:** She shows herself to me with her hands over her heart) *receives your words, your songs, your poetry. Through and to my heart my love, through and to my heart.*

F:
I started to take piano lessons but had to stop—too busy or tired to practice. Too bad.

L:
That's OK, Frank. We can't do everything we want to on Earth because Earth is confined by the restraints of time and space. Someday, if you want to play the piano, you will have ample opportunity to do so. It is just a matter of time (pun here . . . get it, Frankie, time on Earth but not really where I am in the Afterlife). Besides, you make music with your head, your thoughts, and your love which carry a certain vibration that is your trademark, with a unique stamp that is

Frank's alone. A quality that is YOU, Frank. Keep talking to me and spirit . . . your voice, your thoughts become as music. They have a cadence and a rhythm!

F:
When I come to you, can I take you to Germany, to the town of the first known Lutz family?

L:
Let us enjoy where we are now in the present, in the moment. Once you "get here" we will be quite busy with all sorts of activities. But if we do go to Germany, I can tell you I will be the one taking you (along with help from spirit), not you taking me there! (**E:** She laughs.) *I am the one to arrive here first and therefore have acquired more experience than you. Here's a secret though . . . here in the other worlds, if you want to be somewhere you just think of the place and there you will be. This takes some getting used to and practice, but it can be done. You see, this world is so much more dependent on thought and emotion than Earth is. We still have bodies that are just as material as is Earth's but they are made from a finer material. So much finer, in fact, that in some ways it is our thoughts and emotions that have the most influence on the world around us, relative to the body. Over here, it is the reverse as of Earth where it is relatively dense. On Earth, our bodies are like an element which we must work through to live and experience life on Earth. Here it is not nearly as dense as on Earth. This is why it is often a challenge for many newcomers from Earth; while on Earth they did learn and understand why non-material/spiritual aspects of Earth life need great focus. It is easy to forget this while on Earth in an Earth body. It is also easy to get carried away with the material side of Earth . . . but I digress from our conversation.*

F:
Besides visits to Paris, Italy, Germany, and China, what other countries have you visited?

E:
(I hear the word *"Berlin"* . . .)

L:
I've been around the world... Really, there is so much to explore here in my new world! Every day I experience things that are impossible to express with human worlds. You know Frank, our two worlds have a lot of similarities... things are not THAT much different. On the other hand, there are some significant differences. And these significant differences can be breathtaking. Like something out of Star Trek. Like things you simply cannot imagine without experiencing them. It is so beautiful, amazing and there is so much love. There are countries here, in the other worlds, to visit! Many are reflections of countries, towns, villages, and cities on the Earth... Earth's spiritual version. People sometimes will even hold onto their familiar customs, clothing, communities in these "stations". And then there are those places that feel like they are from a beautiful but strange science fiction movie. The buildings and things about such places are just so different. They are very futuristic.

F:
I am keeping very busy, but I still struggle with a lot of depression. Can you see that?

L:
This is what concerns and worries me, my love. The depression you are experiencing. Of course, we all know it is understandable and even predictable given the circumstances. But knowing this doesn't make it any easier for you. We (meaning myself and spirit people working with me) will try to send you communications that have a sense of humor and of a lighter matter to lift your spirits.

Part of the depression is the sense of feeling a loss of control over what happens in life. You were always so dynamic, and still are my love. But on Earth we cannot control the march of time which in this case means it was my time to transition to the next world. It was as if something were torn from your very fiber. That cannot have been stopped or prevented. BUT... accepting that will help you to live in the present now, to feel with your heart that all things under heaven happen for a reason. It is all in divine order. And when the time is right, you too will have a change, a transition. In the meantime, do your best to live in the moment.

We... there are so many of us... are cheering you on.

E:
(Linda shows me herself literally holding Frank under his arms, keeping him up.)

L:
You are loved by many Frank . . . both here in spirit and on Earth. In spite of your sense of aloneness . . . you are not alone. You are helping many others by spreading the great news that life continues after the change called death. You are learning how to experience heaven on Earth through all your efforts and work to communicate with me, all your spiritual studies. Even your thought-forms that have resulted from your readings, classes, mediumship sessions, discussions, etc. are sent out into the atmosphere like radio signals, influencing others to become more aware of the non-material worlds. And when they become more aware of these worlds, their understanding about life and death, how death is not death but a rebirth into the other worlds, this greater awareness will give them courage and hope and even wisdom.

You have a wonderful mind, Frank, one with many years of studies and experience. Keep working with me and spirit so that your thought patterns are either directly shared with others and/or sent out into the ethers for others to pick up on.

Here is something to perk you up: Remember me in my bikini!! Ha . . . that will make you feel better.

E:
(Linda shows herself to me walking along a beach in a yellow bikini with her back to me.)

L:
Remember party time!

F:
What are you doing at home besides painting, music, and writing poetry?

L:
Exploring my new home! So many new things to experience and explore and learn about. We also have meetings that we can go to where the person running the meetings talks about philosophical matters or has guests come to talk about the same.

E:

(Linda is impressing me with something about talks in the spirit world that are related to the medieval time period; something that both she and Frank are connected with. I also hear the word *"Renaissance"*.)

L:

You should see the libraries and places of information over here. Nothing is hidden . . . history as we were taught is often times retold with very different versions. Nothing is hidden here.

F:

Have you seen Alberta, Jim, and my mom and dad lately?

E:

(I hear Linda say the word *"Occasionally"*.)

L:

Yes, I meet up with many including those you ask about. I feel them through my heart and with great love. But I am also making my new life here with many activities and wondrous things. We are all part of one great community, like a big city!

F:

What would you like me to do to help you, when I come there?

L:

Haha! (**E:** I hear Linda laugh.) *Let me help YOU . . . you will be the newcomer!*

E:

(I see Linda shaking her head and then putting her head in her hands and laughing.)

F:

Have you seen on my dining room table the large round Happy Birthday buttons with your beautiful face on them, for the crowd who will be at your birthday celebration at Beyond Baroque, on Saturday, April 13th? We will give out the first Linda J. Albertano Fellowship prize on that day.

L:
Yes of course I have seen them. (**E:** Linda is laughing now.) *So long as it helps others by encouraging them to become poets, participate in the arts, to develop themselves as human beings, to bring hope and happiness to others . . .*

And don't forget to save a piece of cake for me! I will taste its "essence" from a more spiritual context. "Happy Times are Here Again!" music . . . play the music and I will dance to it. Upbeat happy music with drums!

03/20/2024

F:
I'm sorry if a couple of times our conversations have been interrupted recently—it's been very busy here in my place with our book and plans for April 13th at Beyond Baroque!

L:
As much as I appreciate your saying this to me, I am already aware of this. You see, where I am here in the spirit world, we often communicate telepathically. That is normal for us. (Though if needed, especially for newcomers, we may use our mother language to communicate.) So, I am aware of your thoughts of frustration even before you are aware of them. There is no need to apologize. It means things are dynamic and in movement.

I love seeing you so busy and excited about the upcoming Beyond Baroque function and our book publication. I, and others, here in spirit are celebrating these activities. There is a joyousness about them (though I am also aware of a sense of bitter sweetness, but that makes it all a deeper experience). I can see the energy in the atmosphere around you as it vibrates at a higher frequency. The interruptions are to be expected. That is part of the unpredictability of the Earth experience. It would be so boring without it!

E:
(I see Linda making a funny face as she seems to reenact doing something to distract Frank while she was on Earth. Like a kind of a personal joke between Frank and Linda. Something that is between a closely connected couple.)

F:
Your book is about to go to the printer—it is spectacular and beautiful! 220 pages of your poetry and photos of you in action over the years, and some of my poetry, and newspaper articles about you.

L:
I couldn't have done it better myself and I am so grateful for what you have been doing on my behalf. A lot of work has gone into the making of this book,

and I am eternally grateful . . . haha "eternally grateful" from the great beyond. I hope you picked out decent photos of me where I looked decent and not as if I just woke up or something.

I am still loving poetry, and I am so intrigued by which poems you choose to use. Any poem (or pictures or newspaper articles for that matter), are truly fine by me. But there is something personal and special about a written piece of work. It comes straight from the person's heart and is not reliant on a reporter's point of view of what to say nor by a photographer's skill. In some ways, I feel as though the poetry helps you and me to connect more closely when you are reading it or even simply thinking about it. It captures my essence, my energy. Here in spirit, life is not as physical as it is on Earth as we tend to rely more on our emotions and thoughts in connecting with others. So, in that sense, when you read my poetry, your vibrations are easier for me to connect with from here in the spirit realm. (**E:** Then she jumps up and down at the thought of the book going to the printer.) *How exciting!! Frank, you are the best dear!*

What I am hoping for is that someone who reads the book is inspired to pursue poetry, too. Or if they are a struggling poet or artist of some sort, after reading the book this helps give them that bit of encouragement that they are missing.

E:
(Linda shows herself moving among a crowd of people, looking to "touch" the hearts of some of them, those who need a spiritual kind of touch to motivate their creativity.)

F:
We are expecting a big crowd. I hope you can come on April 13th!

L:
HA! I wouldn't miss it for the world. I will be there my love. You can count on that. Watch for the signs.

E:
(I see a large bird flying in the sky, over Beyond Baroque. I cannot make out what kind of bird it is, just that it is large.)

L:
I am going to see who can sense me when I am there! This will be a hoot! And I will have other people in spirit helping me too. This will help to get out the word that life does indeed continue after we transition. The spirit world never wants to miss out on an opportunity to connect with us on Earth.

F:
Cynthia Mellon sends you her love, misses talking with you. And other people ask me about you.

L:
And I of course send love to her too. I miss talking with her also, of course I need not say that. But we will be able to connect again, someday, when the timing is right.

E:
(Linda now shows me her face, she looks about the age she was when she transitioned, but not sick. Her face appears soft, "gentle", and kind as she shows me how much she misses Cynthia. I then hear Linda say the words "my dear Cynthia." Also, the words "not too soon but not too late" we will be together. "We will all be together" and "a gathering of friends and friendship, here and hereafter." "It will be beautiful, you wait and see.")

L:
I can feel when my old friends ask about me. I either feel or hear it directly, or sometimes through you! You sometimes act as an intermediary for me. Like a "conduit". You couldn't have done this a little while ago. So, all your efforts to communicate and connect with me are paying off! Your sensitivities have grown as have your spirit communication connectedness.

F:
What is your latest project?

L:
Thinking about you Frank! Haha. Well, I never stopped thinking about you, so I suppose that doesn't really count.

E:
(Linda shows me herself painting a picture of the people at Beyond Baroque; like a precognitive picture of what will happen. I see people smiling, especially several women, while some are a little teary eyed. There is a sense of excitement in the air as they anticipate what will happen. I have the sense that some are hoping something magical will happen, like a sign from Linda. This seems to mean a great deal to some, like they need validation for a sense of comfort and healing and courage regarding their own lives. There is a sense that the Beyond Baroque celebration will make Linda come alive, as if they can sense her there. They are thrilled. Many are seated. The colors are bright and vibrant . . . reds, yellows, blues. The painting has an almost cartoon-like quality to it. It is like something out of *The New Yorker* magazine, perhaps.

I then hear Linda say, *"I'm working on it, Frank, you wait and see. We have some surprises up our sleeves."* And then something about it being a grand performance, something she has never done before. I also hear a woman's voice singing, presumably at the Beyond Baroque festival.)

F:
Have you done any travelling lately?

L:
I'm too busy preparing things with you, working with you with all you are doing! My travels lately consist of visiting you, mostly through thoughts and emotions. It is wonderful to be able to do this! I feel so light and airy. No worries, no pains, no suffering here. I feel young too!

E:
(I see Frank leaving his body [as in an out-of-body experience] to go someplace with Linda in the ethers.)

L:
Frank may not be aware of doing this, but this is where we are now. We are able to do this occasionally together. I take Frank places he has never seen before!

E:
(I then see Linda moving through the air/ethers; it looks like she is swimming.)

F:
Please tell my parents I love them, and I'm very glad I chose them to be my parents!

L:
They already know that and of course they love you terribly! They are so proud of how you have conducted yourself after my passing. In spite of your terrible suffering and depression, you kept on moving forward with all the projects you have gotten involved with. As well as reading, reading, reading about mediumship and related topics. You've taken all your energy and managed to channel it into higher thoughts and activities. As if you've transmuted the negative into the positive! What a brilliant thing.

E:
(I hear Frank's father say, "*That's MY son! Mastering his own self. Brilliant.*" Frank's mom shows me her smiling face, a face of joy and pride. Frank's parents bring with them a sense of peace, a knowing that everything is OK. That the drama Frank has participated in while on Earth, he has played his role brilliantly. Exactly as he was supposed to. "*We can't ask for more than that, from our perspective.*")

F:
Please tell me one more thing that is fascinating about where you are . . .

L:
When we move from place to place, we can think of where we want to go and we are there. Or we can make it like we are flying and get there that way "Fly the friendly skies . . . " Or, we can simply walk it with our legs if that is what we are most comfortable with.

F:
One more last-minute note I will add later today—outpourings of love for Linda, from many of the 60+ guests I have invited for April 13th.

Linda, I, Frank, have personally contacted over 60 of our and your friends via email and/or phone about April 13th. Almost all of them have said or sent me, or will send me, the most loving comments about you, and they all miss you. Some of them (Suzanne, Ce-ce, Sue Hayden, et al.) have written long beautiful letters about you.

L:
I literally feel those letters as they write them to me. Their efforts have not gone by unnoticed. Their letters do reach me. That is because of their hearts . . . their emotions are pure and carry their feelings and thoughts along to me here in heaven. It is truly a beautiful place, where there is no judgement. There is just love and acceptance of oneself and others. Their letters have been healing for me. And healing for them too. There is nothing to fear about the great transition for it is as natural to life as is being born on Earth. We are just shedding our cocoons and being born in the spirit worlds. We are free from suffering on Earth. We have new bodies of a finer material than what we had on Earth. It is like shedding a worn out, old coat that is very heavy.

I love you, Frank, and I am so proud of you. And grateful for all you are doing on my behalf.

E:
(I mentally thank Linda for working with me to prepare these notes. Linda replies cheerfully to me, *"looking forward to tomorrow's session. It will be fun as it always is!"* Then I hear the song "Aquarius".)

E COMMENTS:
This particular transcript was prepared the evening before. This is unlike the usual routine when transcriptions are prepared the morning of Frank's session.

F COMMENTS:
As you can see, the conversations keep getting richer, no matter when we have them. Always loving.

04/02/2024

F TO E:
This first item may be difficult for you to convey to Linda for me. If so, we can either amend it, or eliminate it, not a problem.

F:
Linda, do you hear me talking to you when I walk up Speedway Alley, past 11 Wavecrest, to get my car?

E:
(Linda hears Frank say that.)

L:
I always hear you dear, when you talk to me. It doesn't matter where you are because time and distance and physicality are non-issues to me. What matters is where your heart is . . . because it has always been with me, it is with me now. Emotions are not physical things, like a car or a given point in time. Your state of mind and intent are what count. Are your thoughts full of light and full of love? If so, then I hear them. It is as if there is an invisible barrier that which prevents you from seeing me or sensing me. However, for me, I can reach through that invisible barrier as your thoughts and emotions carry on over to me.

E:
(I am shown Linda standing in front of a wall. The wall undulates like water, in fact, the wall is transparent like water. She reaches her hand and arm through this water-like wall that is not water, when she hears Frank calling her, talking to him. It is a seemingly strange image, but one filled with beauty in a very strange way. I can see Linda's hair, shoulder length and light colored like blond. She is wearing loose pants and shirt, something very comfortable. She shows me sandals on her feet. She is smiling.)

L:
I know that the U.S. will be experiencing another solar eclipse next week. A lot of people will be reacting to the energies from this in different ways and it is possible that it might seem that connection with spirit is a little more challenging.

Especially when the thoughts of some, that go out into the ethers, are filled with crazy ideas, fear, and so on. If you should experience this, remember that it is temporary and will pass. Remember it is not you but something from others. Don't let it faze you. We will still be with you, all of us . . . just a bump in the road.

F:
It is always bitter-sweet for me, happy memories, sad that you are not with me. I understand that your life is now free from this environment, and that you seem to be doing better than I am doing, but you miss me.

L:
It is sad for me too, Frank. (**E:** Linda sighs.) *But it is the way it has to be for now. It is the way of things, of the order in the universe. I await your arrival! You can count on that. For you it may seem so far off in the future as you are subjected to time on Earth. For me, it is different as we don't have that same sense of time. We are not subjected to the same forces and influences that abide on Earth. Because we don't perceive time in the mechanical way it is perceived on Earth, (for example, 24 hours in one day as Earth turns, rotates on its axis). Time does not seem to move as slowly here, in the spirit world. Things happen when they happen. We can see, to a much greater extent than you can, precognitively. So, we aren't as inclined to worry or feel anxiety about the future. The present is apparent as is the past and future, there is a greater sense of it all happening at once. That's not exactly what I mean to say, but something like that. In short, we are more comfortable with living in the present than people on Earth are. We see souls come and go here, people being birthed into Earth and people birthing into heaven. Yes, I use the word heaven because it is convenient to do so.*

You are doing so much on Earth right now, so many good things that are helping others. Your life on Earth right now counts! Don't you forget that. Your thoughts alone are helping to spread light which is so needed.

I am close to you Frank, closer than you can perceive at this time. Even though I am in this world, I have never really left you. That's because love never dies. Love has its own vibration, its own force, its own substance even if that substance cannot be measured mathematically or scientifically. Love survives the great transition, it survives physical death. That is why our connection continues even though I am in this world and you are on Earth.

F:
Your book is beautiful beyond words! I hope that you can see it!

L:
Yes, you can assume that I can indeed see it. I cannot believe the work and time and effort you have put into this project.

E:
(I see Linda clutching the book to her heart.)

L:
All on my behalf . . . but also, this is helping others. It shows to them how love can survive. That one can still honor those who have passed over in a variety of ways that keep the bond strong. To keep the inner flame of love that never is extinguished. A mother may lose her son in a war and yet she keeps on living on Earth, having a life. As painful as it is to her, she keeps her flame for her son going. She does so tenderly and with great love. And he in turn, remembers his mother communicating on those occasions when the veil is thin enough for him to send signs. And so, it is, with us, my dear Frank. Look for my signs in nature, in small events that normally would be missed, in your own perceptions and sensations.

F:
I have personally sent out over 70 emails about your afternoon celebration at Beyond Baroque on April 13th.

L:
This is beginning to look like the party of the century! Be there or be square, as they used to say. I need not remind you that of course I will be there. The energy will be high and light and beautiful. Remember to celebrate the joyous aspect of the occasion. Many are looking forward to the event. It will be filled with beautiful people all looking for inspiration in some form or another. Let there be laughter and smiles and happiness! You know, with all those people coming together, they just may be like a very large generator making things that much easier for me and other spirit people to send some sort of message

or phenomena. Especially with those attendees who are naturally more sensitively tuned into the world of spirit and non-physical things. It will be like a kind of experiment where we will see what we can do to connect with everyone! Lots and lots of great energy that we can use and work with. We are doing our part on this side of things to prepare. How exciting! Not in my wildest dreams, while on Earth, would I have dreamt of such possibilities.

F:
I have sent an invitation to Jean-Pierre Boccara.

L:
I don't think there is a person on the invitation that you have missed! It will be wonderful to see him come and participate in the festivities.

F:
Have you been on any trips lately?

L:
I've stayed close to "home" for some time now as I have so much to keep me busy here. Truly, my experience on this plane of existence is constantly presenting me with new things to explore and learn. And I keep meeting new people, many of which are connected to the arts in some way or another. And talk about music! Sometimes we get to listen to music played by those who while they were on Earth were well known. Going back hundreds of years in at least one case.

Rock and roll music has an interesting aspect. Here, sometimes the musicians change their music into something of a higher vibration. So even though there may be a certain amount of rock and roll style to it, it has "incorporated" a more cosmic color. Even if it is the same song, it comes across as more ethereal, lighter and of a finer vibration. If a player tried to do otherwise, it just wouldn't work. They might find themselves temporarily in another place more conducive to that kind of vibration!

F:
What are you concentrating on now—writing or painting?

L:
Lately more of the painting though I have not given up on writing, not at all.

E:
(I am impressed with the idea that Linda is working on some kind of artwork that will be at the Beyond Baroque celebration. The people [Earth people] may not be able to see it but they will sense it. Also, this artwork will help to raise the vibrations of everyone. One almost gets the impression that this is a joint effort between spirit people to experiment and observe how the people at the festival are affected. It may be a good way to help us on Earth. They seem to be especially interested in seeing the effects on artistic types because they are generally more sensitive and perceptive.)

L:
Watch and listen to the presenters who will be reading poetry . . . they may be inspired by us in spirit and therefore may seem to stray from what is written. That will be our influence. Or they may show emotion or affectation in the way they say the words, thereby demonstrating that spirit is influencing them.

F:
Leslie, Rob Levy, and Des Walsh all send you love and hugs. I'm constantly hearing from people or running into those who want to know about you, even people who never met you. I tell them how wonderful you are, and how lucky I am.

L:
Awwww, that is so nice that they have not forgotten me! Though knowing how the world of Earth is, I would never blame them if they did. It is very easy to get caught up in the physical world's dramas.

I feel them in my heart. If you can, please send them my love and spirit hugs. If only they could see how wonderful it is over here, I think their reactions might be more of envy. Well, I don't really believe that. It is just that this new world of mine is so beautiful, and I wish I could share with each and every one of you, but most of all you, Frank. It is so peaceful and sweet. There is so much love and kindness. We are both lucky to have had one another. And we still do, as death can never really separate two people who love each other.

F:
Have you seen my mom and dad lately, and your mom and Jim, and if so how are they all doing?

L:
Yes, of course. We do connect but each one of us also have our own lives to live here too. Because we all have different interests, we spend a lot of time pursuing our own interests, just as we did on Earth. By the way, my mother looks so young now, actually everyone does. It is the way of things here. The more we adjust to this world and let go of Earthly attachments, the quicker our new bodies morph into a version that is younger and healthier.

E NOTE:
The following were notes taken before Frank's session, while I was preparing through meditation. The words are from Linda to Frank:
"I'm here, I'm here to help you."
"Not to worry, it will be all right."
"I'm here to help."

During Frank's session, the following communications came through. I communicated them to Frank in real time, as I was experiencing them:

E TO F:
I am being impressed that Linda knows how difficult this has been for you. She wants you to know that she's there for you working on your behalf, with her "people" as I hear her say. "They" know the situation and are well versed in helping bereaved spouses on Earth. I hear Linda say that *"It is not uncommon."* Also, that your parents are helping too but they're not the "experts" she is referring to.

"You are not alone" in your grief. It's something they are (a group of spirit people) working on to better help Earth people with grief.

I now see a man briefly stepping forward who I am not familiar with. He reminds me of Nostradamus, however, I am not saying that he is or he is not Nostradamus. This man is here to work with Frank. This man has an Alchemical connection especially when working with emotion and the human aura. I also see him wearing a dark robe with a headpiece that is pointy. It could be a hat or a hood. He is holding what looks like a crystal ball. Then I see him with a book that he is writing in. I hear the word *"Transcribing"*.

Frank asks if I know the name of the Italian town Linda visited, a small coastal town where she writes. The only name that I sense is the word *"Calibria"* though Frank states that it is pronounced and spelled differently: "Calabria".

04/17/2024

F:
Since we had the big Linda event this past Saturday at Beyond Baroque poetry venue here in Venice, I am gearing several of the later questions toward that event:
   Can we go back to France together when I come to you?

L:
Frank, if that is what you want, then we will go back to France together. However, it is not quite that simple. For when people of Earth first arrive here there is a process they must go through in order to acclimate. Often there is a gathering of family and friends to greet the newcomer. And that takes time but often brings great joy to many. Long awaited reunions of those with deep connections, long bonded by love. Some you will meet soon upon arrival while others will connect with you after you've settled in. It is like a new birth in a new world.

Sometimes, depending on the individual spirit, it is necessary that they spend time in what on Earth might be called a hospital. Those who have passed unexpectedly, suddenly and violently for example, often need special help from not just family and friends, but from those here in spirit who specialize with their trauma. Other individuals may have been sick a long time or suffered emotionally a long time. This would be not of their own doing of course but as one of the hazards that Earth can present. In such cases, a long rest or even sleep may be appropriate in order for deep healing to occur. Such individuals may have extensive understanding of the afterlife but due to unfortunate circumstances, their being or essence needs a deep rest before they can begin to adjust to their new world. The variations on the different situations that people bring with them upon entering the world of spirit are almost infinite. Each case is unique.

One thing is for sure, one's body goes through a transformative process so that their new body develops into health and beauty. Old age morphs into youth, into a state in which the person feels most comfortable. For most people that is in their mid-20s but this can vary. For example, there are some that feel more comfortable with how they looked in their 40s. This process can be very short or very long, it all depends on the individual being.

Once the initial stages of regaining health, obtaining rest and healing have occurred, then comes a period of adjustment and learning. This new world has many similarities to that of Earth's but there are some major differences. As you already know, our sense of time is very different. It is so different that for all practical purposes it is often best described as there being no time here (for those on Earth). However, there really is time, it is just so different from what new spirits are used to.

This world is very mental and emotional. Spirits can sense the emotions and thoughts of others. Sometimes these things even have colors associated with them.

E:
(I am presented with a vision of colors in the aura.)

L:
It can be disconcerting at first to many when they first arrive. But here is a piece of advice . . . try to take it with a sense of humor. That will help to keep your vibrations up and make it a bit easier.

New spirit people often arrive with a number of attachments associated with Earth that need to be let go of. For most of us this may be easier than it sounds because this new world is not conducive to such attachments. Other times one needs to work on it.

This long discussion is to point out that, yes, we can go to Paris together but until the conditions in us both are at a point that it would be safe and "desirable". I need not remind you that there are places here that are spiritual replications of cities and places on Earth. We have a spirit version of Paris for example as well as other places in France and other countries. These spirit locations would be more plausible for us to visit as they are not as dense as is Earth's France. The people are still the same.

F:
Will you still be there when I come? And will they know I belong to you?

E:
(I see Linda yawning. She is sitting with her legs stretched out, wearing comfortable slacks, and smiling. Then she looks at a watch on her hand.)

L:
Of course I will be, silly! I wouldn't miss you for anything. It is love that will ensure I am still here. The love we have for each other. I wouldn't miss it for the world, my dear!

Your question " . . . will they know I belong to you?" in a way makes no sense because there is no one person or group of people in spirit that will be directing you to me or me to you. Source, the infinite intelligence, that intangible and indescribable thing will bring us together. Just as a bird knows where water is, a hummingbird knows where there is nectar, a flower knows how to grow and blossom . . . by the order of Great Nature those who belong together are surely brought together. The love bonds we have are like homing devices. This is a fact. By our own spirit will we be brought together. The law of vibration and attraction teaches us that like attracts like, and so that vibrations naturally attract similar vibrations. Even our thought process which traverse the ethers to each other serve to connect us. Our emotions are like the sweet perfume of a flower, furthering leading our non-physical senses to know where the other is. If this were not so, then how can parents be reunited with their children who have passed before their time? Or children be reunited with their beloved parents when they transition?

F:
Have you heard of a lady scientist named Sonia Rinaldi who can take photographs of people who live where you live, and we can see those photos here?

L:
I did not become aware of her until you did. But now that I know about her, I will with the help of my own spirit people here, do my best to connect to her people! These advances being made on Earth lately are so exciting and it is wonderful to be a part of it. We had heard (in the community I reside in) of some very interesting things going on in the world of spirit that have to do with Earth communications. Around here we are a pretty artistic group, as the more scientific ones are a different community. But there is a lot of overlap! Earth would not be able to do the kind of work Sonia Rinaldi is doing if it had not first happened in the world of spirit. Earth is a kind of reflection of what goes on here in this world. So many scientists here have been

working hard to create connections between the two worlds. Sonia is one of those special people on Earth who is working with us here, to help make that happen.

Just as on Earth where there are artistic communities, business communities, entertainment communities, and so on, so are there a variety of communities in the worlds of spirit. And just like on Earth when the various communities combine together for a common goal, so it is like that here in spirit.

E:
(I am being impressed with the idea that spirit will try to work with Linda's artistic/creative side such as singing, poetry, I am not sure which, when they try working with Sonia. Then I hear the words *"A golden opportunity to try something new, an experiment with this project"*.)

F:
Were you at your party last Saturday at Beyond Baroque?

L:
Well of course I was my dear! How could I miss that? It was very touching to me. I loved it. All this fuss over little me . . . incredible love. All because of my Frank, this happened. I love you so and always will. The vibrations were high at the event which made it easier for me to connect with it and be there. I could feel the love everyone gave to one another. It was truly beautiful.

E:
(I am being impressed with a great sense of pride on Linda's part towards Frank especially, but also towards all those who helped make this event possible. In addition, a great sense of "gratitude" from Linda.)

L:
Your parents were there too.

F:
Did you hear me read my prose poem about you?

L:
Yes, I did, my dear one. And while you read this prose, I was able to blend in even closer with your auric field. It was a blessed event indeed. I could feel our love even more deeply as I blended even more closely with you. I believe that some attendees were able to sense this, even if only on the unconscious level. Though some may have sensed it consciously.

E:
(I am being impressed that one or two people, who were "especially close with Linda" sensed the connection between Frank and her during his recitation. This person(s) would have had some knowledge or understanding of Afterlife communications and would be familiar with how this works. They may not want to talk about it because they may think it is their imagination.)

F:
Did you hear Suzanne and the others read your poems?

L:
Yes, of course, of course, of course to every single person who read my poems. It was an incredible sense of oneness with them all. They did a wonderful job, and I did my best to blend with their auras to influence them as they read. Hopefully parts of my personality came through them as they read. I felt that it did. None of this would have been possible had there not been so much love on everyone's part. Love is what made this possible, this blending of auric fields and connecting with us in the world of spirit.

E:
(I am seeing some spirit people, in addition to Linda, who are helping those on Earth in preparing for the event. Also, these spirit people will be attending the event to continue helping.)

F:
Did you see everybody wearing the button with your picture on it?

L:

You mean my mug shot? I thought it was thoughtful and kindly that they were wearing it. I did laugh at first to see so many walking around with my face on a button. I kind of liked it to say the least but it was a bit strange to me. Almost like I was running for an election. My wife Linda, the mayor. (**E:** I sense Linda laughing.) *Vote for Linda. This is a riot.*

F:

Did you see Gary and Cyd there? They send you their love. Patty, Geri, Staretski, Susan Hayden, Kennon Raines, et al., were there for you!

L:

Yes, yes, yes!!

05/01/2024

E:
During my pre-session meditation and before working on Frank's questions, I saw a crescent moon with its lunar terminator (the line dividing the light part from the dark part of the moon) facing west/to the left. The crescent moon began to turn until its lunar terminator faced east/to the right. Then a tunnel of bright white clouds full of light appeared. As I type this, I am being impressed that this represents a connecting to the other world. A coming together of two worlds, yin/yang, male/female, a blending of the spirit world and Earth.

F:
Linda, I'm sorry about the Sonia Rinaldi photo idea, but I understand, so I wrote to thank her for her interest in you. She sent a very nice note back.

L:
Frank, you being you, try all you can to communicate. Don't doubt yourself as you have come a long way in working towards our communications. The progress is immeasurable. When the time is right, it will be right. You would not be you, if not for your trying out different things. That's what makes you so unique. Don't stop trying and learning. Sonia may unfold at an unexpected time in the future . . . it just doesn't feel right at the moment. That can change. Life changes, as do situations we are in, here or where you are. There are many things you cannot see but which I can from my vantage point. Things you are not aware of, you are not supposed to be aware of. That is OK, that is the way it is supposed to be.

Sonia has many people she works with, hundreds at any given time from all over the world. We might get lost in the fray, so to speak.

E:
(I am impressed with the feeling that as time, as measured on Earth, goes on, Linda will become stronger and at that point a Sonia experience may make more sense.)

L:
I don't want you getting caught up in the crowds, so to speak, at least not now. Everybody is wanting attention, jostling to be in front of the line. Things may get crossed up and confused.

I want you to know how much I appreciate all your efforts to connect with me since I transitioned to the grand world of peace. Haha . . . do you like that name I made up for "the other side"? I'm trying to reinvent this vocabulary. (**E:** *I feel Linda laughing.*) *Everything has a timing and a rhythm. You don't know unless you try and look into things. For now, let's let Sonia rest. You have so much more to do!*

F:
Your Linda Book 2 is going to be beautiful! Alex, Deb, and I are working on it.

L:
I am so excited for this to happen. For "little ol' me".

E:
(I am being impressed with when Linda performed for Alice Cooper. Though I am not sure if this makes sense.)

L:
That's a splendid team you have working on this piece. Your sense of artistic style is playing a large role in this production. I can count on you to piece together the painting in a way that is most pleasurable to the viewer to behold, in this case the painting being the book. I do come by when you are working and interject my ideas, from time to time. It is beautiful (the book). Remember to take breaks as needed, not to tire yourself out.

E:
(I am sensing psychically, the scent of flowers, possibly roses. I am also feeling/sensing excitement over the efforts of Alex and Deb; these are very positive feelings from Linda towards the team working on the book. Also, a sense of gratitude coming from Linda.)

F:
I'm proud of you—per usual—and your beautiful poetry will become a part of American national poetry archives!

L:
You have no idea just how much this means to me. And then again, maybe you do. I have dreamed of this my entire life. It is such an honor. None of this, not a single piece of this would be happening were it not for you, my love. From the start! You have been there for me. My whole life changed for the better. If not for you I would have been nothing. You make my life shine. You brought light into my world. Everything we did together made a difference in my life. You even brought my mother into the picture.

E:
(I am being impressed with the idea that Frank and Linda were responsible for Linda's mom being able to live close to Linda later in her mom's life.)

L:
You make wrongs right.

E:
(I see Linda teary eyed and feeling "beyond grateful".)

L:
Now to compose myself.

E:
(I now see Linda in front of a mirror, putting on makeup as if for a performance/appearance in which she will look "glorious". I hear the song "Betty Davis Eyes" playing in Linda's mind. Then I feel the energy changing into something less emotional.)

L:
You know, Frank, that over here we also have archived poetry, literature, fiction, and nonfiction writings. We have duplicates here of what we wrote/produced while on Earth. I am quite proud of my own collection.

In addition, people here also write poetry and other forms of written art which can also be archived. It does not end just because we have transitioned. The learning, studying, practicing, creating, art, science, literature . . . all continues. It is a beautiful place.

E:
(I suddenly am impressed with the presence of Frank's parents.)

FRANK'S FATHER (who was a scholar):
Frank, I taught you well about the importance of poetry and the more subtle pleasures of life on Earth. Poetry makes it possible for people to connect with spirit, for it comes from the heart. It is a taking of words and creating a painting or picture, if you like, or what one wants to communicate. But done in such a fashion that the reader, indeed, to begin with the poet, is projected into another realm. Words are no longer mere words, but have an energy and power connected to them that when read, can change the individual's vibrations to a higher level. A glimpse into heaven, so to speak. It is the human way of going beyond the five senses into subtleties not available to ordinary speech. It is as if a gift from the gods themselves, to be able express feelings and thoughts with words that dance in synch with one another. This tender way of communication makes civilization, civilization. This for even a straw hut to a castle to a pyramid or palace. It is universal.

F:
I have been thinking of Suzanne and Laurel Ann. They are becoming little old ladies. They always talk about you, how much they love you and miss you, your dinners and movies together, and they really love your poetry. You and I have done well over time. I was thinking I could give the two ladies a gift from you, of something helpful, and a card that I would sign for you. What do you think?

L:
You know if we were both on Earth together, we would do this for them. It is so difficult, so many struggle, especially later in life. This would mean the world to them as well as to me. What sense does it make if friends with means don't help out friends without means? Please give them a nice present. It would mean the world to them and to me.

E:
(I sense Frank's father stepping forward into my awareness. Frank's father likes the idea of helping out Suzanne and Laurel Ann.)

FRANK'S FATHER:
We know that you aren't doing this to receive heavenly brownie points. And therefore, the gift is that much more meaningful. It is true Christianity, what Christianity is supposed to be about. Mind you, I'm not talking about converting or praising the church. It is just that, there are universal ideas about love and service to others that all great religions are supposed to practice. From our perspective, gifting, when done from the heart is something that all who can, should practice. What service has one been to others? There are many forms of service, and in this case treating Suzanne and Laurel Ann is very appropriate. You are passing the love around, so to speak.

F:
What is your latest project? Please don't take too many trips to France or Italy before I get there—I don't want you to get tired of the great food and not want to return . . .

E:
(I see a canvas for painting.)

L:
I am working on art for a while. I feel like I need to paint and draw to express and heal. I can project my emotions and thoughts onto my work, onto the canvas, in a way that I cannot do while on Earth. It is a mode of healing here. The pictures come alive, they vibrate. Almost like a movie but not quite. There are others, Spirit Guides or healers . . . however one likes to refer to them. They can come by and see my work. Then they can see what I need healing on.

E:
(I see a Rorschach inkblot.)

L:
I paint "me" onto the canvas and through that "me" they can work on healing my emotional pains in a way that is more gentle than directly talking to me, assessing me psychically, or so on. These guides are exquisitely sensitive and they can sense and address all sorts of things this way that is safer for them (not as likely to absorb my pain) and safer for me (the canvas is not as direct and has a protective quality so I am not overwhelmed.) Besides . . . it is fun!

E:
(Now I am seeing a musical instrument, the African harp or Kora instrument that Linda learned to play while in Africa. The feeling impressed upon me is that music time is time for fun, recreation, and a different kind of healing.)

F:
I miss you so much, and that's never going to change! I continue to study Afterlife communications, hoping that I will get better at connecting with you there. Have you been able to hear me well lately?

L:
I miss you too, my love! And it pains me that we cannot communicate as easily as we did while I was on Earth. The differences between the two worlds, yours being denser than mine is, makes it more difficult for you to hear me than for me to hear you. But this doesn't mean we cannot communicate. And we do communicate. You just are not always consciously aware of it as I am. You have to work through that physical body of yours, in addition to your own emotions and thoughts.

For me, not having a physical body, it is like second nature for me to perceive the thoughts and emotions of others. My new body is finer and does not filter perceptions as yours does.

Because our love ran so deep when we both were on Earth, and continues to do so, our relationship continues, albeit in a different way. We are just as bonded as we were on Earth! Literally. Love does not die just because the physical body does. Love is its own and is not tethered to physical restraints like the body is. Our love is strong and so are our bonds. Nothing can break that. Often, we communicate while you sleep . . . you just don't remember. While sleeping, those in physical bodies are more open to the psychic world which in turn opens them up to more communications with the world of spirit. Memory is a funny thing, is it not? It is dependent on time and since time is different here in spirit, it should come as no surprise that it is more difficult for those on Earth to remember communications during sleep or in fact, to even be aware of communications taking place while completely conscious. The unconscious is where many communications occur and that is why Craig Hogan said that as soon as you sense something, hold onto it! It happens so quickly it can be easily missed.

But I digress from my telling you how much I love you, always have and always will. And I am here for you no matter the circumstances, no matter if you sense me or not. What's more, there are others in spirit also around you, not the least of which are your parents, but others too.

F:
Linda—just one more thing: If you are OK with it, would you mind contacting Leslie again, just to say hello? She would be thrilled! I think it is easier for you to contact Leslie than me, like you did before. If you don't feel up to it, that's OK too. Either way, I love you, big time!

L:
Yes, of course I will contact her though the success is not up to me. The conditions between the two worlds must be just right. And she may or may not be able to hear or sense me. Actually, I am connecting to her more than she realizes as she doesn't always catch it. These communications are so subtle that they are easily missed. But I will try and do so with something more direct, with less subtlety. Do send her my love! And let her know that I do try to connect with her. Listen to the subtle things in her life.

Of course, I love you big time, too.

05/15/2024

E:
(I can see Linda smiling at me as while I am praying and meditating in preparation for working on Frank's questions. I then hear the words *"settle down"* which makes sense since it was one of those mornings that was more difficult than usual for me to calm my mind.)

F:
Hi my dear Linda—did you hear me read out loud for you from my living room the *In Memoriam* I wrote for you? It is beautiful and will appear in Linda Book 2 of poetry.

E:
(I immediately feel in my physical heart a poignancy that is slightly painful but full of love and longing, coming from Linda, as I read Frank's question above.)

L:
Yes, my love, of course I did. You know I did. How could you not know that I was perfectly aware of this? You are still my "main squeeze", always will be. Here, there, it matters not. I will always be yours. And yours, mine. For it does not end simply because of death of the physical body. It always pains me when you do such beautiful gestures for me as I cannot reciprocate.

E NOTE:
I am being impressed that what Linda means by *"I cannot reciprocate"* is that when she communicates with Frank, in any form possible, that Frank's conscious mind cannot always sense and perceive it. That communications from her to Frank happen far more frequently than Frank will ever know, and that such communications are on a daily basis. But that the physical bodies required of Earth require a great deeper awareness than it does for spirit people. Spirit peoples' messages must be filtered, if you will, through our dense nervous systems. We have been trained to be too quickly dismissive of such sensations and experiences, starting in childhood. This is frustrating for spirit people, but they understand how it is difficult for us.

One reason for this difficulty is to protect Earth people. The most important part of the Earth experience from the perspective of spirit, is volition. Free choice. For that is how we learn. So, the ability of spirit to commune with us does not come easily lest their communications interfere with our volition. Otherwise, the child will never grow, learn and understand. Earth people will develop too great of a dependence on spirit people and will shy away from making decisions of their own volition.

This is not to say that spirit never has a say or never influences people on Earth. Many, many times they save lives and intervene on our behalf whether or not we know it. They influence us to listen to the deep voice within us. But it is done differently than the way people on Earth normally communicate with each other.

(At some point while writing this, I suddenly saw a flash of a woman with brown hair from the neck up. Then, I see this same woman again as she is reading my notes to Frank; this woman smiling at me. The woman looks like Linda but with brown hair, braided and wrapped about her head like something from medieval times. The woman really looks like Linda to me . . . but her hair is darker and fashioned into something from a different culture, time, period. It felt medieval.)

F:
Where you live—did you get any of the solar effects in the sky from the sun recently?

L:
We are protected from the solar effects of the sun. Our dimension is completely different in that we are not subject to the physical effects of such a phenomenon. This is by design of the "Great Spirit". Our sun, our source of light, always shines. It never ends. It is always there. And it is always welcome. We may have periods of twilight light . . . and then most times just bright light. We don't see the sun as you do, as a fixed object in the sky.

However, we are fully aware of what happened on the Earth during the solar event. It was magnificent. We could watch from here what was happening and it brought us great joy to see so many on Earth being touched by the sun's presence. A presence bigger and greater than all. This was by design for the people of Earth. A reminder that there are greater things than the everyday mundane things that most are ensconced in. We rejoiced in seeing the connection with spirit that the lights brought to many.

F:
I will be taking Laurel Ann and Suzanne out to dinner on Wednesday, May 22nd, and will give them your gifts at dinner.

L:
I will be there you can be certain of that. I want to see the look on their faces as I am excited that you . . . well, we, are doing this. Those two deserve our love, they have always been kind to me, never faltering in their efforts. To them I owe gratitude. This is such a beautiful gesture, Frank.

E:
(I see Frank with Laurel Ann and Suzanne, both women are teary eyed.)

L:
They may seem completely oblivious as to what will happen, but they also sense that something is up. Even if not sensing on a completely conscious level. You know, Frank, they sometimes talk to me too! In their thoughts, I hear them. Please tell them that for me. I'm still attached to you all, friends and most of all you, Frank.

F:
Sometimes I talk out loud to you, and you seem to hear me. But most often I try to talk to you via meditation and mental telepathy every day. Can you hear me most every day? I cannot hear you every day.

L:
Every day I set myself up to communicate with you during your meditation. I am there while you meditate whether or not you can feel me. You see, in the beginning of this practice, you are in some ways more likely to sense me because that is our way, spirit's way, of announcing that we are indeed there. But as your abilities increase, our presence becomes more and more

subtle. This encourages you to rely increasingly more on your subtle senses (non-physical), seemingly fleeting thoughts, pictures, visions, sounds. We come forth more strongly in the beginning to reinforce your efforts to connect with us, to encourage your efforts. Then it is required that the meditator, or communicator, opens up more and more to us. Increasingly trusting that those subtle experiences that normally are written off as imagination, is not imagination but is a communication. We are developing your mind to become increasingly more spiritually aware. Also, your heart.

F:
Did you hear me talking to you on Mothers' Day, about the trivial advice I get from friends about how to lead my life now?

E:
(I hear and see Linda laughing.)

L:
Yes, of course I heard you. It is ridiculous.

E:
(I then sense annoyance coming from Linda about the trivial advice.)

L:
Everyone has advice for others, it can be annoying after a while. They mean well but the truth of it is that they don't know any better. They don't know what to say, so they make nonsense of themselves offering unsolicited advice which falls flat. I wish they would shut up. It is folk advice, pay no heed to most of it. People flapping their mouths in the air. Sometimes I want to say to them, to leave you alone, that you have enough troubles to deal with right now.

F:
Amazon and Small World Books are now carrying the first book we wrote about you.

L:
This is very exciting that it has finally happened. I would be happy if just one of those carried the first book, but both are very pleasing. It is amazing how much the world has changed over the years we spent together on Earth. Amazon is global and just through electronics, a writer can reach out to a very wide audience in a very convenient way. It is indeed a small world after all!

F:
Book 2 is also turning out to be a beautiful book.

L:
That is because of you Frank. None of this would be happening without you.

E:
(I hear someone else from the spirit world, not Linda, communicate how wonderful it is that Frank is channeling his grief into creative processes centered around his beloved. How many more people on Earth would be helped by doing the same? It is like a transmutation of grief into joy. A processing that continues the relationship.

    I am also impressed with the sense that Linda was very involved in the production of both books, and not just the pictures, poetry, and stories she left behind. But in an active way, influencing the production process and thereby playing a role from her perspective while in spirit.)

L:
It is not as different as it seems, our separations are not really separate. In many ways, I am still with you even if you cannot sense me all the time. This is what is so hard for loved ones still on Earth to comprehend. It is as if I walked into another room, next to your room, with only a wall separating us.

F:
What projects are you involved in now? I need to know, so I can continue to brag about you . . .

E:
(I see Linda in front of a canvas painting. I also hear the words *"you"* ["you" as in Frank] and *"painting poetry"*. I am impressed with the idea that Linda is working with others who have been in spirit for much longer than she has been in spirit. These others are very interested in observing the communications and projects going on in Earth, Frank's progress in handling his grief, and how his efforts with his books and his learning to communicate with spirit can affect others in a positive way. Linda paints about this in her artwork in spirit. Linda then shows me a painting . . . I can't completely make it out as it is not fully formed in a normal way. But the painting reminds me of something abstract, sort of like a Picasso but not nearly as disjointed as Picasso's paintings are known for. There is a smiling, abstract face on the canvas surrounded by streaks of colors. A bright blue, some red and other shades/colors. The face is sort of tilted and seems happy. I hear the words *"the world of color"*, *"words through colors"*, *"transplanting color"* and *"a world of beauty"*. There is a sense of letting go, of feeling free in the picture . . . almost as if it is an expression of how it felt to Linda when she passed over, during her actual transition as she "shed" her body.)

L:
There was no pain at that point. Much love swirled about me. Then I came to know my purpose in this life. To bring joy and happiness to myself and others in a world with too much cruelty. To let the poet's winged art words fly through the ethers into the hearts and minds of others, to bring upon them the healing of angels in ways unknown, to traverse the mind to places rarely journeyed by those most in need.

F:
I will love you forever—you are the best person I have ever known, and being with you for now 56 years has been absolutely wonderful!! I'm a lucky man!

L:
Now Frank, you know we are both just as lucky. The one for the other. We make one another complete like the yin and yang of life. The one fulfilling the other, the other the one. It is through our love that much is accomplished. We go back in time to another place, where it all began.

E:
(I hear the word *"Roman"*.)

L:
We were, are, attracted to each other because we are similar in our hearts and minds, though it would seem that we came from different sides of the tracks. And is that not part of the point of it all . . . that we came from such different backgrounds and yet love would not be stopped. There is so much more than the material outward appearances of life. Only poetry can express this.

F:
I just received a call from Prince Diabate in West Africa, and photos of beautiful trees he has planted in front of his school in Linda's honor with her name in front of them. I would like to know if Linda has seen the trees?

L:
I saw the trees long before you heard about them. That is because they were planted with the intent of love on my behalf. Those thoughts and feelings traveled the ethers to me, where my mind and heart felt them.

E:
(I see something like a sine or cosine wave traveling through an open area, like space but not space, towards me. I feel as though this wave is symbolic of thoughts and feelings traveling through the ethers. I am impressed that the trees Linda and Frank spoke of have an ecological value, bringing shade where needed, animal life, and a place of comfort for people. A place where someday people can sit under them and play/listen to music.)

05/29/2024

F:
Linda—per your suggestion, I found your ring and slippers in boxes in the studio and put them both on the table in apartment #31.

L:
Thank you, Frankie, I knew you would do that for me. It is just nice for me to know they are there, a kind of comfort. If you are ever moved to do so, you might try chatting with me at the table in apartment #31. The vibrations from my personal items might serve you in being able to connect more easily with me, sort of like psychometry. This is one of the reasons that religious people sometimes pray to a sacred statue as there is a vibration associated with that religious relic. Not that my ring and slippers are religious relics! I am too naughty for that (**E:** I hear Donna Summers's "Bad Girl" playing in my mind.) *All kidding aside, they tell me there is a kind of science behind all of this. And at our stage, props wouldn't hurt us in connecting.*

It is interesting, because I do have personal items here in spirit that are the counterpart of personal items on Earth . . . like those slippers and ring. These items are there for me so long as I need them. At some point, as I develop and become more and more adjusted to this beautiful new world, I won't need such items. They presently serve as a kind of comfort to me. But as we stay on in the world of spirit, we understand that their purpose just doesn't make sense in the world of spirit as they did while on Earth.

Another note is that my spirit items that are the counterpart to the same Earth items, in some ways they feel and are experienced exactly as they were on Earth. But in other ways, the energies are different. I can actually differentiate between the energies of my Earth items and their spirit counterparts. The Earth items have a sense of density to them. If I try to move them, it is not so easy as they are somewhat inert. It is much easier for me to move around my spirit ring and slippers. These are less dense, vibrate at a higher frequency. They are made of a different material than they are on Earth, and since this material is less dense, well you get the picture. Just a little science for you today . . .

F:
I also checked out local art studios, and went to one called Stern, but it was closed, and they don't answer the phone; will go to another.

L:
Take your time. Yes, I am aware of your checking out the art studios. I like to walk along with you when you visit such places. I will try to find out which one is open and influence you to go at the right time so you can catch someone there. Stern may have been closed simply because it is not the right place, or the right person may not have been available. These things are hits or misses. You know how artists are, so temperamental, including their office hours. They have a different perspective that likes to be very flexible and open, including their hours. Can't box them into a schedule. It is part of their creativity.

F:
Did you hear me read to you the beautiful poem and commentary about you and me by the poet Nridgette bianca? She read it at the Beyond Baroque Gala last October.

L:
Of course I did, my dear sweet man. How could I have not? It is indeed a beautiful poem and piece of commentary, to be certain. Everyone seems to know and understand how much we meant, and continue to mean, to each other. I was there when she read it at the Beyond Baroque Gala. And, of course, again with you, when you read it to me along with the commentary. When you read these kinds of things, they are of a higher vibration than the normal daily Earth activities, so of course I would be able to sense and hear it.

E:
(I am given a visualization of the words that Frank read to Linda, moving upwards and into the ethers, into the other world where they are "caught" by Linda's hands.)

L:
When you do those kinds of things, like reading to me, not only am I aware of it, but it is like a gentle, sweet buzzing vibration that I sense, carrying with it meaning through words.

E:
(I see a bee flying about and buzzing.)

L:
A beautiful collage of words and meaning and emotion, a beautiful ballad as if sung during a different time period, in a beautiful court; for the energies of the words are strong and are carried by your intent, while your intent is energized by your love.

E:
(I am given a visualization of an inner garden court, with many flowers and some benches intended for sitting. There is a water fountain. Frank is standing and reading words like those described above. There is some kind of music in the background, which I can't make out except that it sounds like a single instrument.)

F:
Can you hear me talk to you out loud from my living room?

L:
Of course! (**E:** I feel this is stated emphatically.) *You are with me more often than you are consciously aware of. Your presence to me is not being made from the same material I am made of in the world of spirit. Also, your presence often comes to me in the form of emotional and thought-energies. You wouldn't want to be of the same material as I am, at least not yet and for some time to come! But yes, I can hear you talk out loud to me from your living room.*

Talking out loud to me is good "so long as the neighbors don't hear it" (**E:** I hear Linda laugh.) *Words have a power in them that few in the modern world understand. It is the intent and the love that carries over those words to other worlds. For love cannot be restrained by the mere difference of different worlds.*

It is of a higher vibration than anything imaginable. That is the nature of love. It can do anything!

F:
Also, I try to contact you with meditation every day. Sometimes I can't get through. Can you usually hear me?

L:
Yes, I can hear you, of course. But that is OK when you can't get through for we are always there. Not just me, but others as well. Parents, guides, friends. Sometimes I am alone with you, but communications are always done best with a group. The more spirit people that are helping me, the stronger the connection. Though having others around is not always the case and yet we can still connect. Another way to look at this is that in spirit our awareness consists of more dimensions than when we are on Earth. This is because we are not confined by the density of Earth and Earth bodies. In your case, you have to work through your dense brain, not mind but brain, and the general density of the planet. This slows down your vibrations/frequencies. Every now and then, your vibrations/frequencies go up, through deliberation or spontaneously for whatever reason. When your vibrations/frequencies increase, it is easier for you to become aware of us . . . as well as other subtle beings.

F:
I—you and I—took Suzanne and Laurel Ann out to dinner a few days ago, and I gave them your presents. They were thrilled!

L:
I was there, Frank, I was there! It was so much fun and a pleasure for me to see their faces. You don't know how much I appreciated you doing this for me. I even followed them home for a bit, because the energies made it possible for me to do that. There goes that thing we call "love" again! It is wonderful! Please tell them, next time you see or talk to them, that I am looking out for them as best I can from the world of spirit. I have not forgotten them. I think this will give them a sense of solace at this juncture in their lives.

F:
Are you writing poetry these days? What else are you up to?

L:
Yes, but I am wanting to work my words of poetry through you, Frank, so you can write them down. Maybe things about the other world . . . people so need to hear about that today. And, of course, love poetry for you my dear.

Still painting, as described in past sessions. It has become a bit of a passion for me. Music of course . . .

Visiting with friends and family. Everything is so peaceful and loving here . . .

F:
I love you. I'm thinking of getting a Helio Courier airplane and flying up to wherever you are . . . Elizabeth can give me the directions . . .

E:
(I hear Linda laughing.)

L:
Well, one of these nights I may just be able to bring you myself to visit a tiny bit of the other worlds. I will be your GPS. Elizabeth might get lost (**E:** I hear Linda laughing again.) *Besides, I hear she is busy with her own nightly astral travels. Seriously, Frank, there will come a time when you will visit the astral as that would be part and parcel of your spiritual unfoldment. When you are ready, they will be helping me, this often happens to Earth people when they have reached a certain point.*

F TO E:
Also—you won't believe this— I think I was contacted by a Spirit Guide this morning, as I was in my meditation and just starting to communicate with Linda. It was really interesting!! First time I ever had an experience like it. Good pub story for you and Hubby to tell your buddies . . .

L:
That's because you are developing, and it was to be expected. You are opening yourself up to other realities in a way you never dreamed possible. You are

beginning to stand on your own spiritual foundation. WE are so proud of you! This is an important milestone. There's an entire group of spirit people whom you have been working with, and are wanting to connect with you on a more conscious level. It is so exciting. They view you as someone who not only has the potential to develop psychically, but one who can make a difference in the lives of others in many ways, especially when it comes to understanding life after death, grief, hope, and solace. You are in a perfect position to do this!

F:
Linda, I got you an unusual beautiful new bouquet of flowers. Let me know if you can see them on my dining room table.

L:
Ohhhh, ye of little faith! Of course I can see them! I'm not dead you know! (**E:** I hear Linda laughing again, thinking her pun on words is very funny.) *I still have eyes, you know. They are beautiful! (The flowers.) I like the vibrations they give off.*

E:
(The following was from a communication prior to this morning's session with you, Frank. I am not sure who exactly it was from; it felt like it was a group communication, maybe a guide(s).)

I receive a message from a group of spirit people for Frank:

As your spiritual work and unfoldment progresses, it becomes known in this world of spirit. Consequently, you draw attention to those wanting to work with people on Earth to help the Earth develop spiritually, to bring light to the world of which it is sorely needed. We see your earnestness and your dedication to continue your relationship with Linda. She, too, is part of the effort to work with you. It is by design. Linda plays a pivotal role in this drama as she is the link in your opening to spirit. As painful as this journey has been for you, that is often the case. It is like birth pangs in a sense. As you progress and become more confident in your abilities to connect with Linda and in the knowing that consciousness continues after the body ceases, so will you become increasingly more open to connections and commune with other spirit people. You will understand that working with other spirit people will not undermine your connection with Linda; nay . . . it will indeed strengthen it. We look forward to working with you as you continue to progress in understanding, stature and wisdom. Linda is perfectly content to play her role in all this, an important and considerable role worthy of much credit. For it is the likes of Earth people like you, with whom we work in order to connect with Earth from our side in spirit.

06/12/2024

E NOTE:
Towards the end of my 30-minute meditation, I was impressed with Linda wanting to communicate about her clothing that she owned while on Earth. The following are the thought patterns, channeled to me from Linda.

L:
As our bonds through spirit grow, consider giving some (of my clothing) to charity. Pick some you want to keep and give some to charity. These are physical material attachments, to be let go of in order to make room for spiritual connections and bonds between us. For our love is now one of the spirit and in spirit, two minds and hearts still as one. The physical becomes less important as time proceeds and you and I work towards stronger, deeper dependence on our hearts and minds which are not limited by the density of the physical world. Through our hearts and minds, we fly through the ethers into paradise to experience a kind of love rarely had by those living solely in the physical state. It is freeing, it is like the summer's breeze, gentle movement through our very essence. It is love of a kind that knows not the barriers of Earth. For our love can literally move a mountain. Though small and meek such a force seems to many, it is yet great and immense. It is the subtlety of our love that without special mindfulness, makes no sense to the masses. And yet, in spirit, we have arrived at this moment of peace and compulsion towards union of heart and mind, my love. Never will I leave thee. For I am there always with you, by thy side. The two become one in heart and mind through Spirit (God). Thee and heart doth do we meet, for ours to be eternal.

F NOTE:
As in above paragraph, beings in the spirit world can walk, fly, or imagine themselves to move from one place to another.

F:
Kat Georges is also doing the cover for Book 2—great!

L:
Frankie, we are on our way to stardom in the cosmos. Kat is a great artist and very creative. I feel honored that she is helping us. You know, they are talking about your work, well I mean our work, over here in the world of spirit? Yes, you heard that right. People are all excited about your work on the books, as it will tie in well with messages from the spirit people about love not ending just because the mere physical body ends. Your writing and work will offer hope and inspiration. (**E:** I hear the song by Chicago "You're the Inspiration".) *I'm not kidding. It all adds up, with everybody doing their part to make the world of Earth a better place, a more spiritual place. Keep doing your part.*

F:
I'm trying to talk with you from both apartments #21 and #31.

L:
Yes, of course you are dear. You are a man on a mission! And nothing seems to stop you. No matter the situation. I can see my slippers (**E:** I hear Linda laughing.) *They are a very fine pair of slippers indeed. Kind of royalty. Remember, it is all mental! So, subtle thoughts, that you might otherwise dismiss thinking that they don't count, really do count. They really can be part of our conversations. The more you develop, the more subtle will be the messages. Just go with them. Here's a hint: just try talking to me as if I were there. Keep going on with the conversation . . . you might find yourself saying things that you think are coming from yourself, but in fact, when you look back over it a day or two later, may not sound as much like yourself as you first thought. Subtle variations in your own thought patterns may actually be my "personality" coming through and in that way, communicating with you. It is an art, this work. It can be subtle.*

In the beginning, when a novice first pursues communication with us people of spirit, communication is more often than not, unmistakable, very strong, and not so subtle. As the person continues to grow in mediumship ability, the communications become subtler . . . but they can also be deeper, longer, and more sophisticated. It is less subtle in the beginning in order to encourage the person, to show that their efforts are heard, that it is indeed possible to communicate with us here in spirit. As time goes on, this becomes less and less necessary as the person grows in trust that they are really communicating with us.

E NOTE:
While I was finishing up reading to Frank the above response from Linda, spirit communicated additional information to me. I was not sure if it was Linda or not. I shared this additional information with Frank, as it was received by me. Spirit talked about energy, conservation of energy, and experimentation with energy. Spirit talked about the idea of messages becoming subtler with greater mediumship development; this may be a way of conserving psychic energy for different levels and kinds of communication. Also, that the spirit world is experimenting with different ways of communicating with us on Earth.

At this point in the download of psychic information, I am impressed that the communication regarding energy was probably coming from my father who was an electrical engineer while on Earth. Now in the spirit world, he is doing some work on energy and spirit. My father is saying that they are using light as part of the experimentation. Light is being used as a form of energy. My father shows me that one cannot touch light. You might try to grab light in your hands, but you cannot. I sense something about converting light into something denser than light.

Old-fashioned, conservative scientist-types still cannot quite understand or accept this concept. It is important to understand that many scientists are still coming from a historical perspective in which the world first started using electricity around the late 19th century. For the scientists of that time period, it was just phenomenal to be able to make artificial light as was also the use of communication wires, telephone wires, and Morse code. It is hard for them to understand modern technology like cellphones. Some of these outdated attitudes in understanding energy, still affect scientific attitudes, even today. Nikola Tesla's understanding of such things was different, he was an old soul, and he paid a heavy price. Telsa made an immeasurable contribution even though it may not have been recognized at the time by people on Earth. However, Telsa still continues to influence the people of Earth because had a very powerful mind and when his thoughts would go into the ethers that surrounded the Earth, it really did help make a change. There are many things that go on in the background in the world of spirit that we don't know about.

F:
Can you still hear me when I ride my bike and talk to you on the streets of Venice?

L:
Frankie, after all this time are you really asking me this? Try asking me directly, without the intermediary medium! Then listen to your heart and mind for subtle, or maybe not so subtle responses. Go ahead darling . . . I dare you. (**E:** I hear Linda laughing.) *It's not so hard. You might feel me in your heart or just sense my presence. The sun might suddenly peak out from the clouds, a bird might fly by that somehow is a little unusual, you might happen upon my favorite kind of flower or my favorite color, you might hear music that you associate with me. Stop and smell the flowers . . . there is so much of the spirit world around the people of Earth.*

F:
What's the first thing you want me to do when I arrive where you are?

E:
(Immediately before reading the response to the above question, I perceive the scent of a man's cologne. I felt that Linda was sending the scent as a kind of reminder to Frank, regarding the scent that he wears.)

L:
That all depends on what condition you arrive in. You may need to rest and to adjust to the new world. Most people do need that rest and adjustment period. We will all be there, awaiting your arrival as if you were flying in to meet us. (**E:** I see a plane landing on a tarmac and a group of people waiting inside a building room. The room has big windows so the people can watch planes take off and land.) *Don't worry, you don't need a passport. There are no customs to go through.*

There will be a lot of people wanting to greet you. Family mostly, but of course others. We will be able to spend time alone, together of course. But how exactly this plays out, in what order, I cannot say for certain. (**E:** I see Linda standing, with her arms extended out in front of her for Frank to embrace her. She is wearing what appears to be a long, flowing dress.) *Don't worry baby, I will* *be there. The question is not so much "what does Linda want Frank to do when he arrives" but "what does Frank want to do when he arrives". Just take it as it comes, letting everything happen.*

F:
When you see my mom and dad, please tell them I feel so lucky to know all three of you!

L:
Frank, they already know this, my dear. They feel lucky to have you as a son, do not forget that! We did not all come together and connect on Earth by accident, you know. It was all planned beforehand. Each one of us had a purpose and a role to play in the drama of Earth. It was a balancing act with our different energies combining at different stages of life, to alchemically mold our spiritual development.

F:
Do you remember when we went on picnics to Topanga Canyon and the Serra Retreat in Malibu?

L:
How could I forget? Some of the most memorable moments of my life. We don't let go of such pleasant memories of Earth so quickly as all that. It is the small, pleasant things that I cherish. They are worth more than all the gold on Earth.

F:
Another article is soon coming out about you in the *Venice Beachhead*—wow! Everybody misses you!

L:
It just doesn't end, does it? That's so exciting! (**E:** Linda shows me her peeking over Frank's shoulder as he reads the article; it looks like the article is from a newspaper. She is smiling and her thought-energies are as if she is saying "and you thought I wasn't there when you read it".) *I'm with you all the time*

damn it. (**E:** I hear Linda laughing.) *Why do you doubt? I am there . . . a thousand times, I am there! I love you so much Frank Lutz but sometimes you are a thick-headed putz!* (**E:** Clearly, Linda says this in a playful and loving manner to her beloved Frank.) *I miss everyone too, but it is lovely here and life goes on albeit without a physical body. I feel so loved . . . hard start in the beginning of life but because of you, a very different life as we grew together over the years. And now, that beauty continues across the two worlds for love keeps us together. And love keeps me connected with those friends of ours that we also love so dearly.*

F:
Perchance, did you recently remind me that your favorite color is purple?

L:
I like purple royal . . . it's those "blue-like" colors that are calm and cooling. But yes, you could definitely say that purple is my favorite. Don't let anyone tell you otherwise as you know me better than anyone else does. Some people have pig-headed personalities and can be stubborn. There are a lot of people who want to give you a lot of advice and opinions, Frank. Don't listen to them. You do you. Everyone has an opinion. Bullheads.

F:
How many times per day do you hear me say, "Linda, I love you and miss you"? I hope you are doing well there, and I can't wait to join you! I am happy we are doing these books to honor you.

L:
All the time, my love. The spoken word has a way of reaching me through the ethers. I do love and miss you too. Of course, I am doing well here. It is you on Earth, all people, but for me especially my dear Frank, who warrants worry.

The books you are doing are akin to the art therapy I am doing, as we talked about in an earlier session. Sometimes I paint pictures of you, my dear one. It is a way of energizing our love for each other . . . you write about me, I paint about you.

E NOTE:
(I am given the visualization of Linda talking about her relationship with Frank to a group of people. I am impressed that the importance of love on Earth, the Frank-Linda marriage/relationship is sometimes used as a learning opportunity for those who struggled with relationships on Earth. Especially those who had trust issues, or did not treat their mate kindly as they should have. It is good for them to hear the stories of others, who in spite of their rocky beginnings in life . . . or maybe because of their rocky beginnings with others, had very a successful lifetime relationship.)

F:
Linda, I have spoken with Susan Hayden, who loves your work and you. She has agreed to do a foreword for your new Linda Book 2!! Yippee!!

L:
It is with great pleasure I hear this about Susan as I have always admired her work. This is an honor for me to have her do this on my behalf. It is almost unimaginable how so many have joined in helping you and me both. All of this is very healing for both of us. Sometimes people are not so nice . . . but times like this, I understand how deep kindness can flow from those of pure hearts, like Susan.

06/26/2024

E:
During a pre-session meditation a few hours before the session, I was given the following visualizations:

A farm with two buildings. There is a dirt driveway in front of the buildings. An older man with a slightly stooped or curved shoulders is walking toward the barn. His back is to me. He is dressed in dungarees or denim slacks. (Frank's German ancestor?)

A flower bush of some sort. There is a long stem with thorns and a cluster of purple buds at the end. (Linda's favorite color is purple.)

The side of a road with a small shack to my left. There is a large field behind the shack and the road, which seems to extend far and wide. There is a small tent pitched on the side of the road. (This reminds Frank of his maternal grandfather's farmland.)

A young man wearing a football jersey with his back to me. (At first, I thought it was probably Frank, but later during our session, Frank tells me that his father was also a football player.)

About 30 minutes before the session, during a shorter meditation, I am impressed with the idea that Frank's father wishes me to write the following, for Frank:

> *"We are here to support you, Frank. We are always with you, never fear. We never really left you but instead morphed into a different resonance. Hence, the shedding of our cocoon, like the caterpillar when it becomes a butterfly! And so, it is, and will be, always. One thing is given up so something more beautiful will replace it. We are not gone but live on as thoughts and emotions. Just as real, even more so, than while we existed in a physical body. It is poetry of the mind. We are all so pleased with your efforts to connect with us all through your mind, body and heart. You've really opened up another dimension to your life on Earth."*

F:
Can you see the photo of us from 1970 standing together in front of 11 Wavecrest Avenue, arms around each other and smiling? It's on top of papers on my lower dining room table. Sweet!

L:
Of course, I can! I like it that you have put the photo out on the dining room table. It gives off a nice frequency which helps me to hone in on connecting with you. It also is a reminder of the lovely times we had together whilst we were both on the Earth plane together. That is how I look now . . . very young, full of energy and life! Yes, full of life, it's just that it is life on a different plane so to speak. Here I am!

We are all so happy here, your parents, and yes, mine, both of them. Even my father who has, by the way, changed a great deal. We don't necessarily spend a great deal of time with him, my mother and I, but we know how much he has changed since his arrival in space (**E:** I hear Linda laughing.) *It is wonderful. He had to deal a lot with his own self, to come to terms with what he did while on Earth. And to better appreciate the meaning of love. He had a hard exterior in mind and heart while on Earth but he was deeply wounded and was not able to extend himself beyond his own suffering.* (**E:** I have the impression of a soldier, war, alcohol?) *He had to learn to let go and to trust. This was not easy for him to do. But he got help from spirit people who have much experience in working with newbies who have accumulated some hefty karma. But enough about him!*

Speaking of love . . . as in the love between you and me, Frankie. You more than made up for my lack of fatherly love. You were, and are, my savior! My knight in shining armor. And yet this love still continues today. I think my family difficulties early in my life set the stage so that when I met you, I was so appreciative and grateful for your kindnesses. You really did save this damsel in distress. You did indeed my love.

F:
What are the names of some of the flowers there where you are living?

L:
The same as you and I called them when I was on Earth with you. If the flowers are the same as ones on the Earth, their names will remain the same. Of course, if a rose to English speakers is called something different by Italians, for example, then Italian communities will continue to call a rose by its Italian name. The same for other language-speaking communities. However, the longer we are over here in the spirit worlds, the easier it becomes for us to

communicate telepathically; we do not need to rely on a specific language. We can communicate our thoughts and emotions through thought-energies or emotion-energies, mind to mind or heart to heart, so to speak. It is much faster than using words from a language and can express things, in a very accurate way, in which there are no words for in English or any other language on the Earth. One might call this "mind language" where it is actual thoughts that are exchanged between different consciousnesses. And these actual thought exchanges are not degraded by language. The concept, the essence of what is being communicated, remains pure. For language, believe it or not, can never completely capture the true meaning and essence of a thought-energy. Only experience can do that! And we can experience thought-energies!

This is why it can be so difficult for us to communicate with those on Earth. At first, we rely on the language or languages spoken on Earth. But the longer we are here in the spirit worlds, the more we learn about things that exist here but may not exist on Earth. Because Earth things are limited by the minds of its people on Earth. Often, scientists in my realm . . . or artists, philosophers, doctors, shamans, etc., are working on a concept that we would like to introduce to Earth. It may be helpful for Earth's people in many ways. For example, it may be medical, it may be an understanding of physics or even love, and so on. But if we were to introduce certain concepts, we inevitably face the problem of introducing something that Earth people cannot relate to. It is beyond their ability to grasp because they are restricted by the conditions of the planet. Sometimes, it is impossible for us to express the essence of a concept to humans. If we did attempt that, by the time the message was received by someone or somebodies on Earth, the actual meaning and essence would degrade to something much less significant. It would lose its original meaning. It would be like trying to explain something to a small child when in fact, the explanation can only be expressed with calculus!

This is part of the issue Nikola Tesla encountered. He was one of those rare human beings who could, in fact, understand higher concepts. But should he try to share his understanding with others, others just could not relate. The original and intended concept . . . the concept's essence . . . would be lost in translation.

Which brings us back to your question regarding flowers. There are flowers here that express concepts that would be difficult for people on Earth to understand. The best way to experience the names of such flowers would be to simply experience them. "The flower of the violet flame" . . . that's something that I can somewhat relay to you using the English language.

F NOTE:
According to some scientists in the Afterlife, the above-mentioned Nikola Tesla is working from the Afterlife with the Earth-bound scientist Sonia Rinaldi, Ph.D. I first mention Tesla on an earlier page.

F:
Recently, did you and I talk about going back to Rome together and sneaking into the Vatican (as spirits) so I can finish my research project?

L:
Frank, you know I would be there with you should you go back to the Vatican to work on your research project. Just the mere thought of you doing that would bring me to you. If I am with you so often during your day-to-day living, why would I not also be with you on such a glorious trip to Rome? So, of course you have talked to me about going back to the Vatican together. (**E:** I hear Linda laughing.) *Just because I don't have a physical body like you, does not mean I won't be there with you, my darling!* (**E:** While reading this paragraph to Frank, I sense Linda's thought-energy saying, "I will sneak in there for you," meaning Linda will sneak into the Vatican to be with Frank, if he visits the Vatican again.)

F:
I miss you terribly, and other people do, too. Poets and friends. Is that hard to hear?

L:
It is only hard for me to hear because I am very happy here in the world of spirit. It is a beautiful place as I do not have the troubles that exist for you people of the Earth. All that is gone now. What pains me is that I cannot get people on Earth to understand how much better I have it here than you all do. So many of us in spirit feel bad for Earth people because we know how much they suffer. It is not like that here, at all. There is no disease, we don't age, there is no inertia

like there is on Earth, we are surrounded by like-minded people so there is no division. Although, in the lower realms they tell me it is different. Love rules the day in this world of mine.

So, when I see people missing me, although I understand their pain and also miss them, I have no desire to go back to Earth! (**E:** I hear Linda laughing.) *It is beautiful here in the spirit realm. I sometimes try to send our friends some spirit energy to help them feel better about themselves and their situations. The reality is a much more beautiful world than Earth people can experience as they are limited by their physical bodies in how much they can sense and experience those non-material things. Except that those immaterial things are quite material to us here in spirit . . .*

F:
It looks like your archives could be going to Beyond Baroque—they are excited!

L:
Wonderful news for everyone! That is where my archives belong. As I always loved Beyond Baroque. (**E:** I am impressed with the feeling that the possibility that Linda's archives could be going to Beyond Baroque is the result of a lot of hard work by many people. People who love both Frank and Linda.)

F:
I could not find any Hershey's Kisses, so I got some Trader Joe's Dark Chocolate Bark for you instead.

L:
Ohhh, I love Trader Joe's chocolates . . . Joe's Dark Chocolate Bark is one of my favorites! I will hold it with my spirit hands and taste it with my spirit taste buds. Then you actually eat it, and I will blend with your aura to experience it! Love is chocolate in a pretty box. (**E:** I again hear Linda laughing and then I hear someone singing, "Oh what a beautiful morning, oh what a beautiful day." I also hear "*Frank's tickle bone*".)

F:
How are Jim and Alberta? How are my mom and dad?

L:
Everyone is fine and kicking alive more so than when they were on Earth. You do know that we in spirit are far more alive than you all are on Earth. How ridiculous it is that some won't accept that life continues after so-called death. Death is freeing and being reborn! We are so much more alive here in the spirit realm! (**E:** I hear the song "Couldn't Get It Right" of which lyrics include: "*I kept on looking for a sign in the middle of the night . . .* " and "*I couldn't see the light*".)

F:
How are you feeling in general? You always sound pretty good!

L:
I am missing you but also feel filled with light and spirit! This world is beautiful. (**E:** I see Linda from the shoulders up, with blond hair, looking at me and gently smiling. I hear Linda say, "*Tell him I love him so much and that I will be there right by his side. Just look up!*" The music "Couldn't Get It Right" continues to play in my mind.)

F TO E:
That's it, Liz . . . there is one more question that has nagged me for months, but I don't know if it is appropriate for me to ask. I will ask you what you think, but with no pressure on you. It has to do with her last moments here, and did she have any thoughts about what would happen to her, if in spirit or otherwise, after she passed to the next life? I am not sure if I should go to this question . . .

E:
(Linda gives me the impression that she was very tired and relaxed at the point of passing and simply gave in to let things happen. She is showing me light she saw, and something about grandmother and mother were there helping her.)

L:
It was exhilarating, as I left my body I felt light (as in weightless). I was consumed by the wonder of it all. There was no fear, no hesitation once I decided to give it up. I felt lifted up and light as a feather. Prior to my actual passing, I was, well, concerned may be too strong of a word, but I was thinking about

what would happen to my dear Frankie? And I hope it is OK when I actually pass over. But when that final moment came, I was so caught up in the beauty of it all that all my worries were suspended. Completely melted away. I wanted to be able to communicate to you how wonderful it all was, but we both were not yet skilled enough to do that. But really, I was so ensconced in the moment, in the experience, no pain, no heavy body, just beauty and light. It was almost as if I had no thoughts but had a sense of complete joy and peace and love beyond comprehension.

07/10/2024

E:
During a pre-session meditation, I experienced the following:

I see a man wearing a helmet. The helmet and his clothes remind me of ancient Greece or Rome. I associate this figure or am somehow reminded of by this picture, of the Greek god Hermes. I feel the presence of this figure head is related to communication.

F:
Exciting news—Quentin and I will meet to discuss having a young lady poet at Beyond Baroque to expressively read your great piece from 1984, "Telephone Answering Device"!

E:
(I feel a sense of excitement and joy coming from Linda.)

L:
I think she is a good choice (referring to the young lady). It will be a good experience for her. It will be good for her future. This is helping future poets. Grand.

E:
(I am impressed with Linda feeling excited about working with younger people who want to do poetry. About making a difference for future generations. That Linda is going to try and blend with this poet's aura to affect her heart and mind to see what happens. Linda is hoping her own personality will come through as the young woman poet reads the poem.)

L:
This is also an opportunity for young people to experience how closely spirit people are working with them. The young really need this now, particularly in the present world which over focuses on material things. They need a new religion in the sense of spiritual experiences that are so completely different than how most people understand religion. A new awakening. An understanding that the individual can experience communion with people in the spirit

world without fear of being labeled bad things. That people can own their own spiritual awakenings without having to go through a priest or reverend, without being told what to believe but instead to find out for their own selves! A sort of gnostic experience. It is about time.

This is revolutionary!

So, we start out with small things like blending with the aura of a young poet to help her get into character. She may or may not be aware of what is happening but will likely feel something different is happening. It will be interesting to hear what she has to say about her experience in reading the poem. This is nothing to worry about as she will be completely aware of her surroundings. She will likely feel as though she is simply very focused on my character, that she is in "the zone" so to speak. It will be subtle. We always start out subtle as it allows the human being to have plenty of time to adjust to any changes in consciousness. Others listening may even have a sense of a change of atmosphere.

E:
(I see a group of spirit people participating in this "experiment.")

F:
How and what are you doing? I hope you are doing well. I miss you!

L:
Oh Frankie, I miss you too! And love you so dearly, dearly my love. But as you know things are great here. I continue to grow in spirit, developing my subtle attributes because that is what we do when we transition. And learning how to communicate with those on Earth too. I never realized or appreciated how much I have to offer to others in terms of comfort, support and guidance. But now I am beginning to understand my true nature.

We all help one another here. There is no competition with each other. And those few times that such feelings of competing might arise in an individual, it is readily sensed by others. It cannot be hidden, nothing is hidden not even emotions or thoughts. So, because everything is so clear, so apparent, an individual may quickly realize that their thoughts and emotions are giving off the wrong vibes . . . literally. And that is what it is like in my neighborhood. (**E:** I hear Linda laughing.) *Sometimes, it is rare, some* *people move to another neighborhood so to speak, where others enjoy competing with one another.*

You see, that is how it works here. We end up going to the place where we feel most comfortable, so we are naturally surrounded by like-minded, like-hearted other spirit people. This is what is meant by the concept of building your home in heaven while on Earth. What we do, feel, and think on Earth is literally building our future residence in the non-physical worlds. There is no way around this, no way to cheat! (**E:** I hear Linda laughing.)

Don't worry my love, you will be fine. We will be together. With the gentle people. With the healing people. With the people who care about one another. They are actually with you now, even if you cannot see us as often as you would like. Merlin is here too!

E:
(At first, I am not sure about the name Merlin but feel it is referring to the medieval guide that introduced himself to Frank a few months ago. I then see a man in a medieval-type robe pouring some kind of liquid concoction from one beaker to another. He is in a dark room with candles. He feels a bit like an ancient scientist or alchemist.)

F:
Can you see your ring on my finger? I always wear it.

L:
(**E:** I hear Linda laughing.) *The question is, dear one, can you see your ring on my finger? Of course, I can see my ring on your finger! It is a reminder, a source of solace for you, my love. I wear it for your sake, but I tell you that here in the world of spirit, we view jewelry differently. Our thoughts and emotions can create a gemstone which sometimes people will wear. Otherwise, we just let our thoughts and emotions project what is really true in our hearts. In other words, jewelry is not needed as it is on Earth. It can act at times as a symbol of a spirit person's energy. So hence, my energies are still very much tied in with you. Even if I were not wearing your ring, other spirit people could still sense how attached we are to one another. Our attachments to each other would be all around my essence, around my spirit body, also as*

thoughts and emotions. That is because this world is far less physical than your world.

E:
(I see Linda's ring morph into another ring that is more like an engagement ring or some sort of diamond ring. I feel that Linda is demonstrating how in the spirit world jewelry can morph sometimes to convey different meanings. I see both a white gold band and diamond ring on Linda's ring finger. The meaning of this to me is "solid", "not going anywhere", "I am here", "long-standing relationship", "shines brightly", and a sense of shining brighter and bigger than any Earth-marriage jewelry that Linda may have received from Frank. The idea is to show that her love for Frank is so great that it outshines in every way, any physical object that can be obtained on Earth. That she is still there for Frank in mind and heart, she is there forever like a diamond. I hear the words *"It is symbolic but just as real"*.)

F:
Do you hear me talk to you from my front room each night before I go to bed?

L:
(**E:** I hear Linda laughing.) *Of course, I do, you never stop.* (**E:** I see Linda bent over laughing in stitches.) *Things don't change just because one partner doesn't have one of those dense physical bodies anymore. I chat your ear off too . . . you just can't hear me. You really "yak away" once you fall asleep, even though you can't remember it all. You are not supposed to remember it all. Otherwise, you might want to spend more and more time with us spirit people before it is time! But your heart remembers. We are always here to help you.*

E:
(I then see, for some reason, a jet plane taking off. And hears the words to the song *"but I'll be back again"* and *"oh babe I hate to go"*.)

F:
Do you hear me talk to you when I walk up Speedway Alley, past 11 Wavecrest?

L:
Of course, I do! Can you sense me walking next to you? Can you hear my responses?

E:
(Linda is laughing again because she knows Frank can't communicate that easily. I am reminded that this is often the case with spirit people and their Earthly loved ones. And that this is considered to be quite funny by spirit people. I am then shown a person, a child I think, being blindfolded and handed a stick to hit a piñata as a metaphor of the blindness of Earth people to spirit people and the world of spirit. But that there is also a genuine sense of play and joy in all of this.)

F:
Can you tell when I am having difficulties, or I am sad?

L:
Yes, dear one, I can. It is clear as day to me as I can sense your feelings as well as your thoughts. It is true that those difficult times make it more difficult for us to connect. To me it feels a bit like a "force field" pushing back on me. That is how I might describe it. But believe it or not, I am learning how to work through that density. Spirit people have been helping Earth people who are suffering and in pain since the dawn of time. So, we do know what we are doing. Just leave it to me my love. I am constantly learning and growing. During your times of difficulties and sadness, look for physical signs. Maybe something in nature or an object out of place, or flickering lights. That is one way we can communicate when our loved ones are not feeling well. Another way is for you to settle your mind as best you can and request a connection. You can request it directly to me, but you can also reach out to the "Greater Intelligence" for help to connect. You would be surprised.

F:
Your second poetry book will go to Kat very soon, to design the cover, and lay out for publishing.

L:

Kat is always, always very good at this. I couldn't have picked a better person myself. In hands of gold. She has a way of creating things that attract people which is good. So exciting, another book!

F:

Have you been contacting me sometimes during the day? It sounds like you and makes me happy!

L:

Hehehe . . . it took you long enough to figure this out. Why question? Of course, it is me. Though at some point you may be connecting with other spirit people who also love you but play a different role in your spiritual development. They, we, are moving you forward. You are exactly where you are supposed to be right now in terms of understanding, development, and spiritual progress.

F:

I think often about our times and travel together—you and me—such sweet moments with each other, they all touch my heart, and I so long to be with you again.

L:

I do think of you often too, all the things that make a life, an entire life built and based on mutual love and respect. You made my heart sing like a bird singing to the rising sun. We will be together again soon in spirit time, but for you it will feel a lot longer. That is OK, it is supposed to work that way. For now . . . I love you. I always have and I always will . . .

07/24/2024

E:
During my pre-session meditation, I saw a large heart form, within which were Frank and Linda. The couple were each holding what looked like champagne glasses and toasting each other.

    A little while later I hear the words "*It's just so amazing. Star Wolf*".

F:
Linda, lately have you seen any more people you know from here, or famous people?

L:
One of the things that is practiced here in spirit, is to downplay the names of particularly famous people from Earth. This is to remind us that we are all equal in the eyes of the eternal life intelligence from above. Accomplishments that appear to Earth people to be mighty, may appear differently to us in the spirit world. Remember, we can see and hear other spirit people's thoughts and emotions. An Egyptian might ask if your heart is as light as a feather? This is another way of asking how attached is a spirit person to the things of their Earth experience, those things being of a dense nature and low vibratory frequency. There are many who arrive here having accomplished a great deal while on Earth and having been famous. But once they are here, it is apparent that their motivations for such accomplishments may have rested on those things of a lower nature on Earth. Greed, avarice, control, fame, etc. Did they do all their so-called great works for the sake of the spirit world? Or did they do it for self-aggrandizement? For example, how many religious leaders on Earth took advantage of their high positions for selfish purposes? History is full of such examples in all the religions of the world. The same would apply to any other form of prestigious position including royalty, corporations, medicine, etc. Some of the most accomplished people on Earth have achieved little in the way of spiritual development.

    On the other hand, there are many unknown arrivals from Earth that lived their spiritual obligations with genuine pursuit. Once they arrive in the spirit world, their light shines brightly along with their thoughts and emotions. They cannot hide their spiritual stature even if they wanted to. These kinds of spirit people have managed to fulfill their pre-Earth spiritual contracts regarding what they would experience while on Earth. Many here on my side, seek to learn from such unknowns. Such seekers hope that during their next incarnation on Earth, they are better equipped with wisdom and connection to spirit, so as to not get pulled down into the muddy dramas of Earth.

Once it is established that a person from Earth has indeed spent their lives selflessly serving that which is spiritually greater than themselves, then it becomes possible to meet with such persons. It does not take long to figure out a person's status here in spirit because their true self is apparent through their thoughts and emotions. Also, there is often a kind of a light that can surround an individual; sometimes this light seems to be emitted from the person.

When spirit people come together to meet famous and spiritual beings, or not so famous beings, this is done with both small and large groups. Sometimes individuals can meet one-on-one if it is deemed appropriate.

Here, on this plane, I have seen Mozart and Bach. Both led very interesting lives on Earth. Each composer led a very different life but each also had his own challenges and sufferings to deal with. (**E:** I see Mozart.) *Mozart will sometimes talk about his early demise, of which was known even before he was born on Earth. He tells us that his musical compositions came from the heart as he had what you would call a spirit connection. So, while on Earth, he operated with spirit regularly to compose music. His musical work was done with the purpose of uplifting humanity at a time when strife and turmoil reigned. Some of the most beautiful works of any kind can be created through spirit and in opposition to what is happening in a culture.*

Although not mentioned above with Mozart and Bach, Beethoven, too, worked intensely with the spirit world to create his music. How could it be otherwise since Beethoven was deaf? Mozart's musical achievement was a demonstration of how the world of spirit works with people on Earth. It shows how closely Earth and the world of spirit are to each other.

F:
Have you seen or heard Alex and me working on Linda Book 3?

L:
Of course, I have, how could I not have! I am very close to you, Frankie. Our love has always been so deep and strong, as the bonds of love do not loosen merely because one of us does not have a physical body. It is very exciting for this book to come out. However, it was not something that I could have ever anticipated or dreamt of while on Earth. You, I, and Elizabeth are privileged in a way to be able to do this project. This is not being done on your lonesome. You have no idea how many in spirit are taking part on this project. It is a work of art. For when projects are done in tandem with the spirit world, words and writing have an energy that propels consciousness towards the Greater Intelligence. As you know, you have many on Earth helping you . . . Alex, Deborah, Kat, editors, artists, and so on. But do you know that many more in the spirit world are helping?! Some of these spirit people are responsible for the idea of this book, long before you thought about creating it. My goodness, the two worlds working together. Can you imagine! If only more people could understand and practice this, there would be no wars.

F:
Can you see me touch your photo on my wall, and your chiffon scarves, every day and say, "Linda, I love you"?

L:
I love you too, my dear man. And yes, I can hear your words of love when you touch the photo or the scarf. I hear your words even before you have said them because in the world of spirit, time is not linear. Your body, mind and heart emit your words as thought-energies as you go about your daily activities and even as you sleep at night. I am there with you at rest, my dear one.

F:
Do you do your performance art there?

L:
Yes, of course, but often times it is done more as a therapy for those in need. We are using my experience as a performer to develop novel ways of healing as many who arrive here are in need of support, love, and deep healing of the

*heart. (**E:** I suddenly feel giddy and see a group of children.) I also sometimes work with children. They love to sing, and I teach them how to sing with their hearts and their minds. They lift their voices way up to higher reaches of the spirit world because they are so sincere. This raises their vibrations higher and helps them to heal in that way. It brings joy and happiness into the lives of these little ones. I know it must sound very different to you that I am working with children. But here in spirit, we are not restrained into activities that Earth forces upon us. There are many newly arrived children in need, so I jumped at the opportunity to be able to experience it and I love it. (**E:** I see children of different races including a few that look like they are from Africa. I hear the words "big mama".)*

F:
I took Alex and Bob to Topanga Canyon to show them where to put our ashes. Then I took them to lunch at the Inn of the Seventh Ray, very emotional for me, I saw us there . . . !

L:
I am so glad you are taking out time to prepare for when we have both transitioned. Showing Alex and Bob exactly where to put our ashes will make it much easier for those whose job it is to wrap up what we left behind. The fewer decisions they have to make the better and less stressful for them. But Frankie, you have always been like that, thinking of others. That is your nature. Always the knight in shining armor. If not saving the damsel in distress, me, you are helping others and making their lives that much better. You are a very generous and kind man. And very protective of all.

F:
I feel like you have been contacting me during the day, and if so, can you hear my responses OK?

L:
Of course, I have and can! You know that. I don't know why you still ask such questions. You have been working towards communicating with me for over a year now. This fall it will be two years. So, what do you expect? Seek and you shall find. Ask and you shall receive. Well, my dear husband, that is exactly that

what you have been doing . . . seeking and asking. So of course, I can hear your responses. We're getting good at this thing Frank. No joke. (**E:** *I see Frank and Linda standing next to each other as Linda takes Frank's hand into her hand.*) *One for all and all for one . . . even if there are just the two of us. But the saying still works for just you and me.*

F:
I get tears in my eyes when I walk by 11 Wavecrest Avenue and think about how long and how much we have loved each other.

L:
I know you do my dear. I am right there beside you trying to help you feel better. I give you some of my light to help lift up your spirits, emotions and thoughts. I know how hard it is for you to still be on Earth after I left. But I promise it will not be forever. Sometimes I wish that you could glimpse how we experience time here in the spirit world. Then, having to wait for something to happen would be easier for you as you would be, so to speak, living simply in the moment. You would not think about the past or the future so much. I love you, my Frank. Life can be so hard for people on Earth, at times.

F:
Laurel Ann says the workers at Disneyland have gone out on strike for the first time ever!

L:
Good for them! People on Earth are now finally questioning everything. There is a great shift that is uncovering the corruption of the few. This is very painful for many people but in the long run will lead to more transparency and less suffering. With the internet and social media, and phones that can record videos, it is not as easy to fool people as it was in the past. It is not just Disney but all over the world in various forms, that this awakening is happening. The important thing to remember, through all of this, is that you are spiritual beings in physical vessels. You are more spiritual than you are physical. The more that people focus on their hearts and minds, without neglecting their physical needs, the easier it is to experience joy on Earth.

F:
I will meet with Quentin again this week to talk about your archives, and your wonderful poem from 1984, "Telephone Answering Device".

L:
Brilliant! That poem will make for a very interesting read for people interested in how much technologically has changed since the 1980s. The Earth has undergone tremendous change since then. Changes in many ways, with many more coming, the likes of which most cannot imagine. But these changes will first occur in the spirit world before they take on physical form on Earth.

F:
Did we talk recently while you were standing outside handing out flyers of some kind of announcement to people walking by?

L:
We had a conversation that you felt as if it took place in your head. It was in your head, but it was just as real as if you and I were chatting over coffee in one of our apartments. (**E:** I hear Linda laughing.)

08/08/2024

E:
During my meditation, before Frank's session, Linda sent me the following message:

L:
Frank, we want you to know that when other spirit people come through, I am there too. This work we do in spirit is never alone. For as the one communicates, so do we all. I often come through to you, my beloved, for us to connect and that you know our relationship of love is everlasting. But none of this can happen without the work of others in spirit. So, it's not just me, but also your father and mother, my mother, and many, many people in spirit that you may not even know! This goes beyond us, my love. Spirit is taking the strength of our great love for one another and using that to connect with us. But it goes beyond that. We are the initial connection but there are more connections in spirit to follow.

Please know and understand, that not only am I OK with other spirit people communicating with you, I support that. It is part of your development. It's as if our communications to date are kind of a honeymoon period that eventually must morph and change to incorporate your awareness of others in spirit. It is a lab, a laboratory. This may sound funny, but it is not. For all of spirit communication is experimentation.

So, know, my dear man, that when others come through, I am there too! Communications with your family and Spirit Guides will serve to increase your abilities.

F:
Kat will soon have Linda Book 2 ready for final edit!

L:
Of course, we already know about this exciting piece of news, here in the world of spirit. It is going to be a popular book. I love the title, It All Began With Cherry Soup *because it makes me hungry. That was a great time we had, going out for cherry soup to get to know each other better. I was so excited! You were/are such a tall man and for a woman like me who is unusually tall,*

you were a Godsend. Goodness knew that this simple date would lead to a lifetime, literally a lifetime together. I was just happy to find a tall man but then discovered how much more you are my dear man. Your height was just the carrot to lure me in. Your intelligence and humor. Your sense of chivalry. Your dedication and loyalty. I, coming from such a precarious beginning. I, having learned not to trust people especially when it came to love. I, feeling I was on my own having had my sense of security taken from me for most of my childhood. And then you arrive into my life. Bringing me hope, solace, comfort, and a sense of stability like the Rock of Gibraltar. I cannot begin to tell you how grateful I am for this grand plan that played out in our lives, and continues to play out.

F:
We put an ad for your Linda Book 1 on the Linda J. Albertano webpage and other places.

L:
Yes, that is a good idea. Advertising is a must for any new book, even not so new books. The public won't buy it if they don't know about it. It feels kind of strange to be talking about something so, well, pragmatic and down to Earth while we communicate through mediumship. But that is life on Earth of which the realities cannot be ignored. The LJA web page should bring in interest for the book, it reaches pretty far. I am grateful for your thinking of doing that.

F:
T.K. Major is helping us put more info on your website.

L:
This project just keeps on growing in ways I could never have imagined. But having a website will serve to back up the books. People will become interested in more information and the website can offer them details not in the books. Things like links to any videos I am in whether it is performing on stage or old TV series, movies. People love that sort of thing. In a way, this all has historical value. Historical value in general but also as it pertains to the L.A./Hollywood culture. Pretty cool, Frank!

F:
Are you playing any new musical instruments there? Or, what instruments are you playing there?

L:
The "Obee" (**E:** Not sure of pronunciation, but not an oboe.) *I am looking into other kinds of instruments that were played on Earth but I did not have the chance to work much with. Especially string instruments similar to the sitar. But also,* (**E:** Linda then shows me her playing singing bowls.) *There is something about the Pythagorean scale and human vibration, especially as providing healing and harmony. To function fully on Earth, and of course here in spirit, harmony is very important. The Pythagorean scale can help us and those of Earth to do that. After all, Earth people are comprised mostly of water and water does respond to vibratory frequencies coming from sound. Now here is something to think about. There are other musical scales on Earth other than the Pythagorean one. But there are even more musical scales in the world of spirit than there are on Earth! With beautiful harmonious tones that Earth people can't even imagine. However, sometimes spirit people will send the sound of such scales to Earth people who become completely enthralled with it. But should an Earth person try to repeat that particular music sent to them by spirit people, the Earth person cannot do that. They cannot even remember it. This is because it does not exist on Earth.*

You see, music and mathematics are related. Just as between two numbers, there exist an infinite number of sub-numbers, like between the numbers 1 and 2 there is 1.1, 1.11, 1.2, 1.345, etc. Well, there are an infinite number of notes between two harmonious notes on a scale. In spirit, we can sense some of these in between scale notes because we exist in a finer form capable of experiencing subtleties of all sorts, that Earth humans cannot due to their denser bodies.

Even more amazing is that these numbers, including the infinite ones, have shades of color associated with them. Sometimes when a healing is done on someone on Earth, the vibration and color of a subtle note, that spirit people can hear but Earth people cannot, is used to bring back harmony to the body of an Earth people. It is like a science, but also an art form, a philosophy all wrapped up together! Too bad there is not a word in the English language, or any other Earth language, to describe this.

This is like, as when on Earth, lasers are used for healing. This of course, is just in its infancy of development. They, the laser researchers, have no idea just how far this new healing method will take them. Earth is in for a treat.

So long as we have the desire, we never, ever stop learning in this world of mine. And we so want you all on Earth to join us as much as possible. There is so much love here and we want to share it all with you, my dear love.

F:
Do you know how much I love you and miss you?

L:
Yes, I do, my dear Frankie "boy". A tall Frankie boy too. (**E:** I hear Linda laughing.) But yes, because it is that immense love we have for each other that makes it possible for us to do what most people consider to be impossible. To communicate between two different dimensional worlds. You're doing it, Frank! You really are.

I miss you too. But it is only a matter of time, a long time by your standards of course, but by the standards of the spirit world not so long at all. For we both have had many lives on Earth, that while on Earth those lives felt like an infinity. But, in fact, are not really all that long. Time is so strange in some ways. How can a period of time feel so much longer on Earth than it does in the world I presently reside in? We in spirit are traveling, so to speak, maybe vibrating would be a better word, much, much faster than Earth people.

F:
Do they have barber shops there?

L:
(**E:** I hear Linda laugh.) *Ha! That's a funny but good question. Yes, we do have barber shops for those who feel they need a barber to cut their hair. Once a person gets used to being here, they just mentally decide how long or short, what style of hair, and so on they want. And that is how their heart remains. If they want to change it, then they can mentally change it to what they want. I think that for some people, because they went to a barber on a regular basis while on Earth, they aren't wanting to give up that practice. So, they go to a barber. It gives*

them a sense of peace and comfort as they can't handle too much change in too short of a time. The rest of us, well, we just go along doing our business here in spirit without the need for barber shops, hair salons, and so on. We have better things to think about. Good things that are wondrous and beautiful.

F:
Do you want to dictate a poem to me, to reprint and present here?

L:
That would be wonderful, yes, I would love that. Keep in mind that such a poem may come to you at night, at least perhaps parts of it. You might need to keep a journal by your bed so you can write it down. Then again, you may sit down one day, all settled and peaceful in mind and spirit, and the words just come. We will do this together, I with you. Write down what first comes to mind without thinking about it, whether or not it sounds like me or not. It would be good if your mind were clear and unobstructed from worries and distractions and self-judgements. Just write down what first comes to your mind and worry about it later.

F:
Sometimes, depending on the day, I can't hear you. Can you hear me usually?

L:
I, being a form of lesser density than that of Earth people's, can hear you all the time. You, being in a body that is denser than my own and residing on Earth which has a much denser atmosphere and surroundings, naturally won't be able to consciously hear me at times. But you know what Frank, your unconscious is registering my communications. It is just that the leap from the sub- or unconscious to full consciousness does not always work. That is the way it is supposed to be while you are on Earth. Otherwise, you would be too inundated by sensations and influences, all day and all night long.

E:
(I am being impressed with the idea that in order for Frank to catch/sense a message it is like a surfer catching a wave; everything has to be just right. Also, that a spirit message(s) is like an undulation in the atmosphere.)

F:
Have you been on any trips lately?

L:
Not lately. Staying around here for now in case you want to connect with me. Well, I suppose visiting you is a kind of a trip! And I do get around the place here in my new dwelling. But nothing too unusual in the sense that I prefer, at least for now, to stay here where I feel most comfortable. And it is easier to connect with you from my home base, so to speak. Don't worry though! There is plenty for me to participate in, experience and see where I am. It is a pretty vast region. So many indescribable experiences to have.

F:
I want to improve my clairvoyance, or see you when we speak together.

L:
Remember, my love, that these things take time and have their own rate of development. Keep doing what you have been doing while remembering that when you are ready, you will be ready. You can no more force this to happen than a preadolescent boy can force his voice to change overnight, or his body to grow a mustache. When the time is right, the time is right. In the meantime, we will all be here ready to help!

8/22/2024

E NOTE:

After meditation:
For Frank from spirit (as a collective group):

One of the most important things to remember while working with spirit is the need to remain harmonious. This applies to whether it is inner harmony of the individual or outer harmony when working with others, especially those who are part of your spirit communication circle. In the coming months, there will be great turmoil surrounding politics, not just in America but over the world. This is because there are great changes taking place on the Earth, different cosmic influences, different understandings of what life is about that Earth's people will be experiencing. This has been a long time in coming, the energies causing this turmoil have been building for many decades. Added to all this is the increasing difficulty for leaders of any sort, not just political, but all fields including science, medicine, education, business, etc. to hide information from the public. This is due to greater transparency through technological advances, especially as it applies to the Internet. The people of the Earth have grown frustrated on both sides of the upheavals that are taking place. Their frustration inevitably is sent into the ethers and is felt by others, who then join in with the frustration increasing it even more, which also goes into the ethers, making for a cycle of building anger and frustration. This is nothing new on the face of the Earth for there have always been upheavals of the sort, periodically. It is part and parcel of the Earth experience.

It is imperative that, in order to continue communication with spirit in a smooth and satisfying manner, individuals involved in this sort of work maintain their sense of balance, regardless of what happens outside of their sense of self. For if there is one thing that is most important to spirit communication, it is harmony. Without harmony, communication will become more challenging. The connections between our world and yours is a fragile one that can be easily broken. This you know well, Frank, as your diligent studies, experiences, and practices have taught you this past year and a half. It is now all the more important to remember this, for this is a time period that tests and challenges humanity to remember where they really come from, who is their true source, where is their actual home, what is an illusion, and what is real. Does the individual fall apart and end in with the muck of humanity's anger and frustration? Does the individual pull themselves up, practice self-mastery over the lower self, and rise to the occasion as a beacon of support and light, in a time when it is needed more than ever? So many will struggle with this and become caught in a mire not easy to distance from. But those whose focus remains on source, on the light of wisdom, can and will serve as a beacon of hope for those others who struggle to remember that we all are—not just those of us in the other worlds but also our brothers and sisters on Earth—people of the stars, of the cosmos and beyond.

F:
When you went to Germany, where did you stay (i.e., hotel, or . . . ?) And did you visit the City of Rothenburg?

L:
Hello, Frankie! Well, that was some serious stuff that the spirit group wanted to impart to you. I'm glad I am not on Earth right now (**E:** I hear Linda laughing.) *It is quite the drama taking place over there where you are right now. By the way, I was present while the message was being conveyed to Elizabeth, as I often am. Just to be clear, this message is going out to a lot of people from spirit, as it is needed now. So, it is not so much that you, Frank Lutz, need to hear it as it that all people need to hear it. Spirit is doing its best to get this message out to as many on Earth as will listen. And they know you will listen! We are not asking you to cut yourself off from the world nor to stop keeping up with the news. It is important to be up to date with what is happening in your world. Rather, we feel it is in the individual's best interest to remain as objective as possible. To do more observing and less identifying with what is happening. Look at it as a*

chance to study and learn about the human experience on planet Earth. Since you are not young anymore, even though to me you are! It becomes easier to step back.

Don't worry, if you forget I will be sure to nudge you to remember. Hey, Frank . . . forget it and have a beer! Listen to music. Watch the ocean and soak in the beautiful sun.

OK . . . now to your question about Germany. When we from the world of spirit visit the Earth, we are not in need of a hotel to stay in. Our spirit bodies do not require the kind of rest that an Earth body does. We can stay in a park in the middle of winter and it would not matter. But, because of habit, we usually stay where we felt most comfortable while on Earth. Whether that be in a home we once lived in, a hotel we are familiar with, or a friend's place. But we really don't need a place to stay in like we did while on Earth.

E:
Linda shows me the inside of a building with beautiful, ornate furniture, some with gold that is someplace in Germany. I am impressed that it is either a high-end, historical hotel or maybe even a historical mansion or some other beautiful building. I see the word "1800s". Then she shows me the inside of a more rustic looking place with dark wooden beams supporting the ceiling. It does remind me of a place where beer is served, like a pub or a restaurant. I hear the word *"Bavarian,"* and I see women serving beer in large beer mugs; these women are wearing traditional German attire including a skirt with a white blouse and darker colored vest. I sense a lot of joy and happiness. I can perceive the odor of delicious food, the kind of food that comes from that part of the world.

I am also sensing that Linda did not go visit by herself. I hear the words *"was brought there"* and sense that it was her own mother that "accompanied" her. *"There were others too,"* Linda says. A group of us spirits went. I hear the word *"father and mother,"* and I feel it was Frank's parents. But others in spirit, too. Kind of reminds me of a tour.

F:
Should we give Laurel Ann and Suzanne some more help at some point?

L:
Absolutely. They deserve it. It is not easy nowadays for people to make ends meet. And Laurel Ann and Suzanne were always such good friends. They are still my friends! I want nothing more than for them to be happy and pleased. Any gesture or sign of love is always a good thing but even more so nowadays because of what people are going through. Of course, there are also many young people who are also frightened about the world they are living in. But right now, because of our bonds with Laurel Ann and Suzanne, a little gift from me from the Afterlife would go a long way in providing them some hope, some laughter, some light heartedness.

F:
Susan Hayden is doing a presentation at Beyond Baroque later in September. Do you want me to read to you the beautiful foreword she wrote about you for your Book 2?

L:
Oh, for heaven's sake, Frankie! Of course, I want you to read it to me. Why do you even need to ask? I can feel the vibrations of her foreword already, I am actually drawn to it. I could, if so inclined, read it myself without you or anyone having to open the book for me. But I would so enjoy it if you read it aloud to me. It would give us another opportunity to connect emotionally and while you read it, I will also be able to connect with Susan. Not that I need you to read her foreword to me in order for me to connect with her or you. But, by reading it aloud, you will generate more psychic energy to help me connect with both of you. It is like that anytime a person actively communicates with a spirit person through speech, writing, music, or any other modality. Thought itself, of course always has been and always will be a way of connecting. But speaking and other modalities can sometimes help build up the psychic battery, the psychic generator to make communication all the more strong.

F:
Do you hear me talk to you as I walk up Speedway Alley, past 11 Wavecrest Avenue?

L:
Of course, I do, silly man! Why do you even ask me such things at this stage. Thoughts have a weight that although not measurable on Earth, we can sense while here in spirit. Thought has a quality and essence to it. Thoughts are real things. They are not physical in the way humans understand the physical world, but thoughts have a power and a force behind them. Thoughts are like a gentle breeze that can be felt but not seen. Thoughts can also be like the wind of a hurricane that is so strong it has the power to make people want to take shelter! (**E:** I hear Linda laughing.) *Your thoughts are as of the gentle breeze on the beach coming from the Pacific. Hearing your thoughts is like standing on our beach and feeling the sun warming us and feeling the breeze cooling us off in just the right proportion.*

F:
Do you hear me talk to you as I ride my bike down Rialto Avenue where we used to walk to the Erewhon Market on Venice Boulevard?

L:
Oh, here we go again, Frankie, with a repetitive question.

E:
(I hear Linda laugh and see her shake her head.)

L:
OK, of course I do. But when you ride your bike down the avenue near the market, some pleasant memories come up in my mind. I loved that market area. But I also loved our beach and all the other places around where I lived with you while on Earth. In a way, I still live there because of our deep connection through love. Love is incredibly powerful!! Is it not?

F:
Alexis Rhone Fancher, Cindy Mellon, Laurel Ann Bogen and Suzanne Lummis, and Charles Duncan miss you and send you kisses. So do we all!

L:
Ohhhhh, I miss them too. Someday however, they will be able to join us here in these other worlds. And it will be a grand celebration! One by one, they will come to join us by returning home from whence they came from before their life on Earth. Not a second before their time, though. That is so important to remember. I am so grateful you have been keeping up our old connections with people. And so grateful to each and every one of them that they are still in your life. Please let them know this. Tell them, also, that I miss them too and send them kisses too. And thank them for me for not forgetting you, helping you out, staying connected with you. For if not, well, I just don't know if I would worry about it all the time. I would never be able to settle in here in my new life. What's more, because I would be so worried I would probably not be able to communicate as well with you.

E:
(I feel Linda sighing . . .)

L:
So, yes. Do send them my love, my gratitude, and kisses. Tell them I love them, each and every one.

F:
Who have you met there who is really interesting?

L:
I have met myself. I have seen myself, as myself, for myself, because of myself. I have seen, and felt, and experienced a great connection with a power or a source that is part of me and I of it. This knowing experience has brought me great solace and peace. For in the end, it is ourselves that we have to contend with. Just not in the way that most people understand the saying "for myself". Far, far from that meaning. When we understand ourself, then we understand others.

9/04/2024

E:
At the very start of my pre-session mediation, spirit strongly impressed upon me that they wanted me to trance speak. I recorded the transmission, it is over seven minutes long. See/listen to recording . . .

F:
I made a reservation at the Hotel Bel-Air for breakfast for you and me yesterday, 10:30am. Were you with me?

E:
(Pre-Meditation: I see her sitting at a table with Frank. With white tablecloths. Round table. Lots of lighting in the place.)

L:
Oh, of course, I was with you. You know that. I am always with you. Time and distance do not matter when working with us spirit people. I am always there. Distance is a strange word to use though because the world I now reside in, doesn't have the same concept of distance as do people on Earth. Ours is more dependent on condition. So, while Earth people might ask, "How far do I need to drive to get to Philadelphia?", we in spirit might ask, "How should I change my vibrational frequency to experience Philadelphia?" Yes, we have a sense of distance and when we do, we also have a sense of movement from one location to another. But it does not contain the density that accompanies movement on Earth. Dreams sometimes come close in approximation to what I am trying to describe. The dreamer can walk, drive, bicycle, or fly from one location to another. They may never reach that location during one dream, but in another dream, they reach that location by almost morphing into it and without having to experience every step of the way. So much of this depends on the work of the mind.

F:
It is wonderful for me to have you around me—lucky me!

L:
We are both really lucky, double blessed to have each other. This is not the ordinary way a relationship proceeds after a spouse transitions to the other world. It is because we were both ready for this, after a lifetime of preparation. A preparation, I might add, that we were completely unaware was happening. Focusing on our deep love of one another, we built up quite a strong psychic connection without even thinking about it. We just accepted it as something that close couples develop. It was all so natural, which is the way it is supposed to be. Our experiences since I have moved to a new neighborhood (**E:** I hear Linda laughing.) *have enabled both of us to experience spiritual growth, in a way we never understood to be possible.*

F:
I recently wrote a long prose poem called "This Place" but I think it was your poem. The words had kept popping into my head, I was not trying. Then I suddenly sat down and wrote it without lifting my pen! And in the end, it was a story you were writing about yourself! And you kept referring to me.

L:
See!! This is part of what I am trying to communicate to you. It WAS indeed me. It truly was. There are all sorts of ways to commune with spirit and the mighty pen is not one to be ignored. Didn't it feel natural? That is because that is the way it is supposed to be. It is a god-given right (**E:** Linda laughs at the use of the term "god-given" as religion was not her "forte".) *You see life does indeed go on after death. You see it has to do with consciousness, this is what I am learning. And your consciousness too. All of life, whether it is on Earth or here in the spirit world, depends on our consciousness for experiences. It's all in our heads!* (**E:** Linda shows me herself laughing. She looks like one of the pictures I have seen of her.) *The spirits are in our heads, Frankie. You are in my head just like I am in your head. Two heads are better than one and this proves it!*

    Keep on writing like this, Frank, as this is not the end of your development. Not for a long shot. There will be many more opportunities for you to write about things you cannot even begin to imagine. I am just the start. Yes, yes, dear husband, there will be more poetry and stories coming from me. But others will also be working with you to communicate. And don't worry, you won't become so fixed on writing that it will interfere with your other psychic abilities. Just the opposite. In fact, it will help to facilitate the development of your other abilities. Sensitivities are like that. Think of a daisy plant! First one daisy pops up and blossoms and then another, then another, sometimes more than one at a time. Psychic unfoldment is like that. Just like a daisy plant.

F:
I will be happy when I am able to sense that you are here with me, and I hope I can see you, too.

L:
Why wait until you are here with me in spirit? We have so much we can and are doing with you on Earth and me in spirit, along with many others in spirit. This separation of ours, which really is not a separation at all, was preplanned. Let's both take as much advantage of it while we can. Then when you do eventually transition, we can boast about it to the neighbors . . . and the mayor and the governor and the Pope. (**E:** Linda is laughing again.) *Well, things really are not structured like that here, not at all. Just wanting to get you to laugh and enjoy the time we have with one of us here and the other on the planet. Because . . .* (**E:** Linda draws out the word "because".) *. . . we can. Because it is a golden opportunity to win a spirit Oscar! Not that there are Oscars here, nor is it like Hollywood. Hollywood is not exactly spiritual and not exactly without a heavy materialistic flavor.*

F:
I told Jean Caby that you have coffee with us, and you described the tables to me. He loved it!

L:
And THAT, my dear Frankie, is what I am talking about in terms of making a difference on Earth. Jean may be only one person, but by encouraging his understanding of the continuity of life, now his thoughts, thoughts being real things, can go out into the ethers along with similar thoughts from others. The more correct thoughts that there are floating around the ethers of Earth, the more

people's attitudes and understandings will change in a positive light, about life after death. How do you eat an elephant? One bite at a time, dear!

By the way, I do enjoy joining everyone for coffee. But sometimes it is sooo funny to us in spirit, the way Earth people can be so oblivious to our presence. Sometimes we can see people trying to sense us because they know it is possible and they genuinely want to experience this. But they don't sense us even though we are standing next to them! The truth is, they really are sensing us, but they are trying too hard by using their physical senses to perceive us. They have not yet learned to use their non-physical senses which are so fragile especially in the materialistic world of the 21st century. Also, the non-physical senses are very subtle. Relax, open up, and listen to that deep tiny voice within you without dismissing it as nothing. This is why meditation can be so helpful as it helps people to focus and to be mindful of things they normally don't bother to notice. It is the simplest and most natural thing . . . but also very difficult for the modern mind to grasp. You think while on Earth that technology and contraptions are needed to commune with us in spirit. But that could not be further from the truth. Everyone is born with the ability!

F:
Leslie and Kennon Raines send you love, as do other fans of yours.

L:
This is so wonderful! Perhaps at some point I will visit them and hopefully they will be able to sense and perceive me. But you know what . . . I already know their love, I can sense it without the need for it to be passed along through you. Though I very much appreciate your doing so. I know it because I can sense beyond the four dimensions of life on Earth. And, because love knows no bounds. So, I can sense their emotions as well as their thoughts. Their emotions kind of attract me to them and then I can sense what they are thinking or saying to each other. Love is like that. We, us people in spirit, just want you on Earth to be happy!

F:
What are the names of some of the Afterlife plants you are studying?

L:

Well, names of plants are tricky here. Remember, we have things here in which there are no words for in any Earth language, including English. We rely on telepathy (for lack of a better word) to communicate. Here are some sorts of translations to give you some idea, though the actual meanings are a bit different:

Plant of joy and light, plant that loves to sing, plant that welcomes newcomers, plant that raises vibration, plant of light.

And so, Dear Reader, Frank & Linda will continue their Afterlife adventure, with the help of Dr. Liz. We hope this writing has been helpful to you.

FRANK'S ARTICLE ON GRIEF
AN IDEA FOR THOSE WHO GRIEVE

The main thrust of this document is to help those who have lost a loved one to understand that they are not alone, and that—believe it or not—human and scientific systems are being used today for the living to possibly get into contact with your dearly departed. Furthermore, with training and practice it may be possible for you to learn this skill.

It happened to me: I lost my dear wife Linda, and I learned how to have direct contact with her. I write this document to help you, Dear Reader, and to honor my Linda.

After Linda passed away on September 13th, 2022, I was in shock, severe grief, and depression. I became very busy organizing her various art works and winding down our business. At the same time, I started investigating the process of Afterlife communications. But in late November I received a call from a dear lady friend of ours, Leslie, who lives in Denver, with a surprising story she had to tell me. She told me that for many years on occasion she would hear a voice in her head, usually telling her that some member of her large family was in distress or had a serious health problem.

This particular night she had been asleep, and at 2:00am she was awakened by a loud voice in her head, yelling out her name and my name, and the voice woke her up. The voice was Linda, telling our friend that she had been trying to get a message to me, but my grief was so intense that she could not get through to me. I had read that severe grief could be an impediment to receiving Afterlife communications. So Linda wanted our friend to convey some information to me, which our friend was happy to do. In fact, our friend had written down two pages of notes, based on what Linda had said to tell me.

Our friend faxed me the notes. Linda wanted me to know that she was OK, that she was being well looked after, that the place where she was living was quite beautiful, full of peace and kindness, and that yes, the people there looked human, but had no bodies; they were indeed spirits, but could look completely human, with clothing on, and so forth. And their "minds" (i.e, consciousness) worked quite well, they could think, write, create, etc. Obviously, Linda's contact with our friend and the notes to me were surprising, but I had already started to read about the Afterlife, so the communication made sense, according to what I had been reading.

In addition to my busy days, I started reading voraciously late at night, as I am a fast reader and have a good retention rate. My readings by various authors who were involved in various aspects of the Afterlife science were to give me a sound understanding of what was real, and how it had been proven. In addition to my reading, over the next few months I took various online courses in Afterlife communication techniques, and two courses in meditation, including one in Transcendental Meditation, which I highly recommend.

By early November I had heard about and investigated the process of communication with departed loved ones, otherwise known as Afterlife Communications (ALC). I thought to myself that as desperate as I was to communicate with Linda, she must be equally desperate to communicate with me, after all these years of loving each other. So I decided to start researching what I would come to understand was an intense, widely and deeply studied and researched science.

So I started reading about the science of quantum mechanics and its discoveries since the beginning of the 19th Century as to how the world works on a subatomic level, a key to the development of understanding ALC. I went on to read books by psychologists and parapsychologists, medical professionals, researchers, practicing mediums, people who had near-death experiences (NDEs), and people who had actually communicated with their departed loved ones (DLOs). Between November 2022 and the end of September 2023, I would read 43 books. In addition, in January 2023, I started taking online classes in the science of ALC, instructed by professors, researchers, and mediums with advanced academic credentials and degrees, and who are some prominent names in the science: R. Craig Hogan, Gary Schwartz, Suzanne Gieseman, Kriss Kevorkian, Elizabeth Raver, Hillary Michaelson, et al. I continue to read and study the science of ALC. To date, March 20th, 2024, I have read 57 books on this science of communication.

Now, on to the main purpose of this document: I believe that most people in the world at some point in their lives lose a dearly beloved person, a relative or a friend, and the loss is devastating to them. I further believe that many people would like to maintain contact with the person who they lost, but don't know how to do that, and/or don't believe it can be done. I would like to show or explain to those folks that it can be done, that there exists plenty of evidence to that effect, and that I can explain to them the science and how it works to allow them to make contact. I would start briefly with an explanation of the science that helps to make communication possible, and then describe the process of communication, and finally, what a person must do to be able to partake in the communication.

I also worked with several mediums in order to begin contacting Linda; I have stuck with the two best mediums, both of whom are ladies who are well-educated, and have been doing mediumship work for decades, and are the best at it. I continue reading and taking courses in this science of Afterlife communications.

IN THE BEGINNING:
Early in the 20th century, a German physicist named Max Planck discovered what came to be known as subatomic particles. Later, a Danish physicist named Niels Bohr expanded on Planck's work. Thus, the theory of quantum mechanics had its beginnings. Both of those scientists would later be honored with a Nobel Prize. All things in the universe are made of molecules which are made of atoms and subatomic particles, smaller than atoms. We cannot see atoms; we must observe them with very sophisticated equipment and spectroscopes. As to subatomic particles that also reside inside the molecular field along with the atoms, they cannot be seen either; in fact, only their action or what they do can be seen, as they can be millions of times smaller than their atoms. These tiny items that make up the matter in the world—including you and me, animals, rocks, plants, and so forth—have enormous energy, essentially electromagnetic energy and light. This is all about matter and energy in the world at the most fundamental level. It is claimed by science and physicists that the power of subatomic particles and their electromagnetic energy collectively can be more powerful than atomic energy. And that is all we are, in our most basic form: electromagnetic energy and light.

Why is this important? Because that is what messaging, communication is—electromagnetic energy and light. When we speak in person, when we talk on the telephone, when we talk telepathically, it is all electromagnetic energy and light. Light travels at over 186,000 miles PER SECOND. When a 17-year-old boy on vacation from his home in Germany comes to visit Venice, California 7,000 miles away and gets bitten on his leg by a shark while swimming in the Pacific Ocean and thinks of his mother, she at home in Berlin can feel a message of pain in her leg and sense that it is from her son, instantly. This suggests the message was sent telepathically, or via mental telepathy, which may have moved at least at the speed of light. Science does not yet know whether or not electromagnetism is a good working model to explain the phenomena of telepathy. However, because telepathic messages are often experienced instantaneously, this suggests that telepathic information is traveling at high velocities, similar to electromagnetic transmissions. Intentional telepathic messages from one person to another are the way in which a living human being here on Earth is able to speak with his/her DLO, who is also living, but in an altered or "transformed" form, in the Afterlife, as pure consciousness in a human form. Furthermore, the scientists and professionals who work with Afterlife concepts do not say that when we pass to the next life that we have "died". They say that we have simply "transformed" or "transitioned" into a different type or form of existence, and that we are very much alive and accessible for communication. They also say that we can take on other forms, but essentially our thought processes, our memory, and other abilities are all intact. Why would that be? Because we still have our consciousness, and our thought processes, reasoning, communication skills, and so forth.

The scientists also do not refer to the Afterlife as heaven or hell. They refer to the beings there as spirits; they use religion-neutral language, as just like here on our Earth there are many different types of people and their religions in the Afterlife.

Where do we get all of this information about the Afterlife? Basically, from two sources: from what we call NDEs, or people who have had a Near-death Experience (NDE); and from our DLOs in communications with their loved ones here, as they describe life in the Afterlife. Let's start with the NDE.

Someone in your family may have had an NDE. Let's say it's Uncle Joe, who goes into hospital for a heart operation. During the procedure, poor Uncle Joe dies. As the medical team is frantically trying to revive him, Uncle Joe feels himself leaving his body, and floating up toward the ceiling of the operating room. From the ceiling he can look down on the medical team as they work on him. After a couple of minutes Uncle Joe decides to go back down to the area around his body and try to talk to somebody, but nobody can hear him, so he tries to touch one of them. But his hand goes through the body of the medical person, unnoticed. So then he tries to move the gurney where his body is lying. But again, his hand goes through the gurney. So Uncle Joe realizes something is different, very different. Next, he feels himself floating up toward the ceiling again, and moving on to somewhere else. After a short time, he sees the entrance to a tunnel ahead of him, and he enters it, not under his own power, but rather he is lifted into the tunnel. The tunnel is dark inside, and Uncle Joe feels himself floating forward for a while, he does not know for how long. After some time, he sees a light at the end of the tunnel. He continues to float toward it, until he comes to an end, where people help him out of the tunnel. As he emerges from the tunnel, he sees a group of friendly-looking and acting people who are helping him, including some of his recognizable deceased relatives. The physical environment is described later by Uncle Joe as quite beautiful, much like the Earth and at the same time different. He is there for a while, being treated well and made comfortable. Afterwards, an official looking person approaches him speaking kindly to him. The person gently explains to him: "Uncle Joe, it's not your time yet. Your work on Earth is not finished yet. We need to send you back."

With that, he is put back in the tunnel, and sometime later—the NDEs never know how long these episodes last—he finds himself back in the operating room, lying face up on the gurney, with his eyes just opening, and all of the medical staff looking down at him, happy that he has survived. None of them know about or even suspect the trip that he has just been on.

The research shows that approximately 98% of the surveyed NDEs describe the same sort of experience, worldwide. The NDE experience can vary widely in terms of time the person has this experience; it might last for only a few minutes, or much longer. The longest time a person was "dead" has been witnessed and recorded as seven days, and it happened to an American doctor, a brain surgeon named Dr. Eben Alexander. It happened several years ago, and since then he has written and spoken about his experience. At last report, Dr. Alexander is alive and well and practicing medicine on the East Coast of the USA. What is more remarkable about people like Dr. Alexander and others who have experienced NDE is that even though they were dead for a while, they actually remembered their death experience, and can recount it to professional medical people; when you die, your memory bank stops working. So while you are alive, some of your memory is obviously stored outside your brain, as well as partially inside it. After you are "on the other side" your internal memory bank no longer works.

There are several well researched books about the NDE experiences of many people. I can recommend some of the books about NDEs that I have read.

Now let's move on to what we hear from our DLO's about life in the Afterlife. My own experience in communicating with my dear wife Linda is consistent with the reports I have read about communications between other people on Earth and their DLOs.

So how do I recommend that you start to learn how to communicate with your DLO? To start, I recommend that you learn how to meditate, or take a course in meditation. I recommend Transcendental Meditation (TM). Why TM? Because in my experience it was the meditation style that helped me get my mind the clearest and empty of trash and clutter, as well as allowing me to get deeper into the quiet parts of my mind. I also suggest that you start to read about this science. Of the 57 books on the subject that I have read, I can recommend probably 15 to 20 that were most helpful; but if you are uncomfortable with science, I would not recommend the two books on quantum mechanics and subatomic theory.

During this early phase of your involvement, I also suggest that you start to identify who it is in the Afterlife that you want to contact, and why. I would also recommend that you seek out at least two mediums who you have researched and feel good about, as being persons who might help you contact your DLO. You can research them online, and they do not need to live near you, nor do you need to have an in-person session with them. In fact, the less they know about you, the better. Of my two ladies, one lives in California, the other lives in Connecticut, and I have never met either of them in person. We do all of our work by phone. When you contact them give them the least information about yourself as possible, like, your name and very little more.

More than likely, you will then be invited for a Reading, or a situation where you are on one phone talking to the medium who is on his/her phone, and who will be in a trance-like state that will be an asset to the communication. The medium will then take a bit of time to try to make contact with your DLO, having very little information about your DLO. The medium will be relying on his/her various trained "senses" or a set of trained feelings and intuitive help, in order to make contact with your DLO. This is when the fun starts, because sometimes anything can happen! Members of your family from generations past may show up; your past and passed away pet dog might show up; Uncle Joe might show up. When all this time you wanted only to speak with your old Granny who took care of you when you were a kid. But eventually your medium will make contact with Granny, and the dialogue between you, the medium, and Granny will begin. During the session other people may show up just to say hello. The sessions typically last for about an hour. Then it will be over, and more than likely you will be very glad you did it. And you will be amazed by the whole process.

I believe your next step is to ask your medium, or research it yourself, about a school or instruction as to how you can learn to contact your DLO by yourself. Then you will have as resources for connection to both your medium and you, like I have found to be both beneficial and personally very wonderful.

Recommended books to read, most of which can be bought on Kindle, for a lower price:

Your Eternal Self by R. Craig Hogan

Proof of Heaven by Dr. Eben Alexander

Afterlife Communication edited by R. Craig Hogan, an Anthology

The Crossover Experience by DJ Kadagian

The Intention Experiment by Lynne McTaggart

"Become an Empath with These 8 Brain Training Tips"
by Steve Phillips-Waller
(www.aconsciousrethink.com/2887)

ONE FINAL NOTE TO YOU, DEAR READER:

As I tell people, before my dear Linda passed on, I did not know much at all about Afterlife communications. But after she passed, that topic kept getting my attention. So I surmised, if this is for real, and Linda has found out about it, she must be as desperate to communicate with me as I am to communicate with her. So in early November 2022 I started reading—a lot—about it. By the end of December, I had read 14 books on the subject in nine weeks. By September 2024, I had read a total of 67 books, covering all aspects of this science. In January 2023 I started taking online classes and Zoom classes on the subject, while continuing to read, plus doing various tasks to archive Linda's art and to create a scholarship for poets under her name.

As I have mentioned, I wanted to understand the science behind this communication science, so I started reading about quantum mechanics theory, subatomic particles, and so forth. It was very useful to me, but is not necessary for you to read, to benefit from this wonderful communication system. I also read books by scientific researchers, psychologists and parapsychologists, medical doctors, mediums, and by people who have had NDE experiences and/or have communicated directly with their DLOs (Departed Loved Ones). I also had medium contact with Linda, with the help of several Mediums, and decided early on to stick with two lady mediums, one in California and one in Connecticut, both of whom are outstanding. I work with them over the phone to do Readings (i.e., conversations) with Linda.

Needless to say, I have benefitted greatly emotionally and psychologically from my communications with Linda, both via mediums and directly one-on-one. She seems happy in the Afterlife, as she describes it to me. She has explained to me how she lives there, what it looks like, and what she does, and about friends she has made there, and members of both of our families she spends time with there. I can highly recommend that you look into it, if you lose someone you love, and want to maintain contact with them.

ADDENDUM

What follows, Dear Reader, is slightly outside the purview of this book, because neither of the two events I will describe here, that happened to me, included the presence of Dr. Liz, and only one of them included the presence of Linda.

The notion of After Death Communications (ADCs) between loved ones is widely understood and accepted in most parts of the world; seemingly less so in the USA, but growing at a rapid pace here. Scientific research has added to the acceptance of the reality of ADCs. I feel compelled to apprise readers of the possibility that they, too, might learn how to communicate with their Departed Loved One (DLO), both via a qualified Medium, and/or directly, like I do with my Linda. In my opinion, in order to accomplish the process of ADC requires researching the topic via your own reading, plus tutelage in a classroom or computer online, plus engaging with a medium to at least start your ADC with the help of a professional. The community of mediumship and ADC is widespread and involves researchers and practitioners from all over the world, whose aim it is to help the bereaved, both here on Earth and in the Afterlife, to communicate with each other. In other words, the help we get from our fellow humans here is augmented by those of us who have passed into the Afterworld of Spirit.

The event that occurred to me with the presence of Linda but not with Elizabeth, was a clairvoyant event, a natural occurrence in the Afterlife, although in my case, not frequent. The other event, that occurred to me alone, without the presence of either Linda or Elizabeth, was a visit to me from one of my Spirit Guides, when I was conscious and starting to meditate before contacting Linda.

In the almost two years since I started studying Afterlife communications, I have had more than 15 but fewer than 20 clairvoyant experiences, all of them vivid, all of them with Linda as the subject. I will describe the first one to you.

Since January 2023, I have studied how to connect with Linda with the aid of a skilled medium (like Dr. Liz or Hillary) once each week, and I have studied how to contact Linda directly, by myself, which I try to do on a daily basis. The day that I had my first clairvoyant viewing was in the summer of 2023. I was in a meditative trance, eyes closed, and mentally ("telepathically") saying Linda's name, searching for her response. Unlike her prior responses, which were voice only, suddenly a living, moving picture or scene opened up in front of my mind's eye! How this would happen had been described to me by the researcher/scientist R. Craig Hogan. The scene was in full living color of Linda sitting at a table by her kitchen, writing with a pen on what looked like a yellow legal pad, Craig had told me to quickly react with a word, any word, as soon as I saw something, so I quickly said, "Hi, Linda!" to which she responded while writing, "*Oh, hi!*"

I told her that I could see her like in a movie picture scene, not a still camera photo, and in full color. I told her that I could see her table, the writing pad, the pen, and her, all as though I were present in the scene.

To verify it all, I asked her, "And it looks like you're wearing a white long-sleeved shirt, right?" She affirmed, "*Right!*" and looked to her left in the direction of my voice, smiling. It felt to me as though I were in the scene with her, full of movement and sound, full color, full of life. I was elated, quite pleased, that finally I could see her, and felt like I was present with her, no matter where the scene was taking place.

Since that clairvoyant event, I have had several others, all clear, in color, full of movement by Linda, and in some cases, some of the friends she has made there. She has shown me her garden, the forest near her, the open fields outside of town, a body of water nearby where she went horseback riding, and other places.

I hope to have many more of these clairvoyant events. Now, on to my visit from one of my Afterlife Spirit Guides.

I am not a religious person, but I have always been spiritual (i.e., I have always believed there is something beyond us, another world where our ancestors have gone, and that maybe I will go, too). In Afterworld parlance, there is a strong belief system centered on the existence and activities of

Spirit Guides, and a hierarchy of other members in a spirit world. I have felt, and sometimes seen, the presence of spirits of one kind or another over my lifetime, and in various settings both here at home in the USA and in other parts of the world. But when I started studying Afterlife communications, a whole new world of spirits opened up to me, in my readings, my conversations with mediums, scientists, and researchers, and in my studies. I had been told that I should not be surprised or concerned if at various times some of my spirit helpers begin to speak to me, usually very briefly; they are your friends, I was told. I was also told that it usually is some time—months or years—before you receive contact from any spirits who are there to help you, but they are always aware of you.

One midmorning in early August 2024, I sat down on my living room couch to settle in and start my meditation so that I could contact Linda directly. I closed my eyes and started my meditative breathing routine, an essential for me to have success in contacting Linda. I had not been thinking about Linda or anything else at the moment, as I was attempting to clear my mind of everything. Suddenly from the right side of my closed-eye field of vision appeared a young female, maybe in her mid-twenties, with long brown hair, a brimmed hat on her head, wire-rimmed glasses on her nose, and a smile on her face. What I was seeing was very clear, and friendly-looking.

"*Hi, Frank,*" she said, "*I'm one of your Spirit Guides.*" Surprised, I responded, "Oh, hi! Yep, I'm Frank." Then she said, "*Just came by to say hello.*" And before I could ask her for her name, she disappeared! Later that day I asked a medium friend of mine, and another buddy of mine at the local Transcendental Meditation Center in Santa Monica, California, Denny Goodman, about this sudden meeting. They both avowed that we all have Spirit Guides that help us through life, and that they are the friendly souls of those who have passed to the Afterlife before us.

None of the above surprised me, but I was happy to have these events, as affirmations of what I have read and been told in the past less than two years since I began studying Afterlife communication. I have also been visited on three occasions that I know of by Linda, and in all events she was visible to me. Once was very late at night, and one time was in the midafternoon, both times while I was at home. The most recent time, in the autumn of 2024, I woke up from a deep sleep at about 2:00 in the morning.

I saw in the dark, sitting in a chair about six feet from my bed, Linda, who was looking at me and smiling, I said, "Hi! Wow!" She responded: *"You sleep so peacefully."* We looked at each other for several seconds, smiling, and I looked down for my sweater, and a few seconds later when I looked back up she had disappeared.

But she will return!

Frank Lutz

ABOUT THE AUTHORS

Linda J. Albertano was born on April 17, 1942, in Moab, Utah and grew up in Denver, Colorado. Her mother was an artist and her father was a land surveyor. Later her father abandoned the family and reported her mother falsely as a malfeasant, so the local authorities put Linda and her younger brother into repressive fundamentalist Christian homes, which created an emotional hardship for the kids for the rest of their lives. However, because Linda had a brilliant creative mind, as well as physical beauty, and height, she would go on in life to become celebrated and honored in film, music, performance art, and poetry, following her graduation, *Cum laude*, from UCLA. Linda's passion was the spoken word. When asked by her husband Frank why she became a poet, she responded in a loud voice "Because I want to be heard!"—a response borne out of the verbal repression she experienced in the foster homes as a child. Sadly, Linda passed into the Afterlife on September 13, 2022. We are all lucky to have the ways she expressed herself available to us both vocally and musically. An extensive partial resumé of Linda's work can be found on her web page, **www.LindaJAlbertano.com**. The first page of this web page shows some of the honors she received, and venues in which she appeared, in North America, Europe and Africa. She is the co-author of ***On the Life of Linda J. Albertano***, ***It All Began with Cherry Soup***, ***Two Souls Desperate to Connect***, and ***Poetry Diva: More Poems by Linda J. Albertano***.

Frank Lutz, Linda's husband and companion since 1968, was born in Charleston, West Virginia, and grew up in Ohio. His father was in the automobile industry, and his mother was a part-time artist. He was a talented athlete and a scholar, like his father had been. Frank's father introduced him to poetry when he was ten years old, and only recently has Frank gone public with his poetic works. After having been injured playing football at Ohio State University, he went on to universities in France, Italy and Germany, finishing his scholastic undergraduate work at UCLA, where he graduated *Summa cum laude*, and was inducted into Phi Beta Kappa scholastic society. He was awarded a graduate Fellowship, and today sits on the Council for the UCLA Center for Medieval and Renaissance Studies. He has done academic research at the Vatican Secret Archives in Rome. During his student years he had travelled the world's oceans as a student oceanographer. He also has a Commercial pilot's license. Frank feels that it is a privilege and an honor for him to author and to help Linda publish her works of poetry and prose in the books indicated on the opening pages of Linda's web site. The love relationship between Frank and Linda endures forever.

Elizabeth Raver, Ph.D., is a retired Psychology and Math professor. Her doctoral degree is in General Psychology and her dissertation was on the lived experience of Math anxiety in elementary school teachers. "Dr. Liz" as she is sometimes called, is also certified as an Intuitive Spiritual Life Coach and in Reiki II. She is a member of the Afterlife Research Education Discussion (ARED) online group and the American Association of Psychics and Healers. Dr. Liz has studied mediumship in the United States and Great Britain. She has been practicing mediumship formally since 2007. However, she has been a sensitive since childhood and used to play with "imaginary friends"; it was not until her mid-twenties that she began to understand that she is a born medium capable of communicating with the spirit world. At present, Dr. Liz serves local spiritualist churches by giving spirit messages to congregants, healing and sermons. In the past, she has demonstrated mediumship to college students. In addition, she was a medium participant in The Yale COPE Project. This project studied differences between schizophrenics and psychic-mediums, in order to better understand nonphysical voice hearing. She offers private and group mediumship sessions, classes and workshops. In addition, she does life coaching regarding spirituality and related topics. Her mediumship includes evidential, light trance and energy work. She works with people from all over the U.S. as well as internationally. Sessions are held online, on the phone or in person based on each individual person's needs. When not involved in mediumship, Dr. Liz loves spending time with her husband Richard and their kitty Louie. She enjoys writing, reading, cooking, gardening, music, watching the night sky and Netflix. Additional information can be found on her website, **www.drlizmedium.com**.

BOOKS BY LINDA J. ALBERTANO AND FRANK LUTZ

Quiet Time Publishing is pleased to publish the Linda J. Albertano collection, a trio of tributes to the poet and performance artist, along with work by her husband of 55 years, Frank Lutz.

ON THE LIFE OF LINDA J. ALBERTANO
FROM TRAUMA TO HIGH ART
**By Linda J. Albertano with Frank Lutz;
Foreword by Suzanne Lummis**

On the Life of Linda J. Albertano features photos, memorabilia, images, and performance reviews from Linda's personal journal. But most important is the collection of stories, poems, and provocative prose by both authors.

IT ALL BEGAN WITH CHERRY SOUP
**Poems and Stories by Linda J. Albertano and Frank Lutz;
Foreword by Susan Hayden**

This companion book to *On the Life of Linda J. Albertano*, offers a retrospective of Linda and Frank's written work, including poetry and prose, providing a fascinating look at the creative force that emerged from this one-of-a-kind relationship.

TWO SOULS DESPERATE TO CONNECT:
WITH HELP FROM A THIRD ONE
By Elizabeth Raver, Ph.D., Linda J. Albertano, and Frank Lutz

This one-of-a-kind literary work reveals how two lovers, separated by the death of one, have remained in contact, featuring actual transcriptions of "live" conversations between Linda in the Afterlife, Frank on Earth, and Elizabeth, the Medium who helps them. It offers a guide for readers to contact their own departed loved one directly!

COMING SOON: POETRY DIVA: NEWLY FOUND POEMS AND STORIES

For more details, visit
QUIET TIME PUBLISHING
online at **www.quiettimepublishing.com**
or scan the QR code

www.ingramcontent.com/pod-product-compliance
Lightning Source LLC
Chambersburg PA
CBHW051330110526
44590CB00032B/4470